# William James
# in Focus

D1739254

# William James in Focus

## *Willing to Believe*

William J. Gavin

*Indiana University Press*

BLOOMINGTON AND INDIANAPOLIS

*This book is a publication of*

Indiana University Press
601 North Morton Street
Bloomington, Indiana 47404-3797 USA

iupress.indiana.edu

*Telephone orders*   800-842-6796
*Fax orders*   812-855-7931

Manufactured in the United States of America

Library of Congress Cataloging-in-Publication Data

Gavin, W. J. (William J.), [date]
    William James in focus : willing to believe / William J.
Gavin.
        p. cm. — (American philosophy)
    Includes bibliographical references and index.
    ISBN 978-0-253-00786-5 (cloth : alk. paper) — ISBN
978-0-253-00792-6 (pbk. : alk. paper) — ISBN 978-0-
253-00795-7 (electronic book) 1. James, William, 1842–
1910. I. Title.
    B945.J24G385 2013
    191—dc23
                                          2012031813

    1  2  3  4  5   18  17  16  15  14  13

*For Cathy*

Our mind is so wedded to the process of seeing an *other* beside every item of its experience, that when the notion of an absolute datum is presented to it, it goes through its usual procedure and remains pointing at the void beyond.

—William James, "The Sentiment of Rationality"

# Contents

# Preface

William James is arguably America's foremost philosopher—or at least one of them. But the one thesis for which he became most "infamous" was his espousal of "the will to believe":

> Our passional nature not only lawfully may, but must, decide an option be-
> tween propositions, whenever it is a genuine option that cannot by its nature
> be decided on intellectual grounds; for to say, under such circumstances, "Do
> not decide, but leave the question open," is itself a passional decision—just like
> deciding yes or no—and is attended with the same risk of losing the truth.

Many thought that this kind of psychological subjectivism had no place in the cold logical circles of philosophy, where one sought objectivity and, ultimately, certainty. A strategy was undertaken to engage in some sort of "damage control," that is, to allow sentimental concerns in "soft" areas like morality, interpersonal relationships, and religion, but not in the "hard" areas dominated by the sciences. The present study argues for the opposite of this position. It suggests that the will to believe should not be relegated to specific domains; rather, it should be em- ployed wherever choices between options are "forced, living, and momentous." It also argues that the will to believe is not a onetime affair but must be continually reaffirmed in life.

Going further, the will to believe has presuppositions—metaphysical presup- positions. It can function only in an unfinished universe—"wild," James would say, "game flavored as a hawk's wing." It requires affirming the type of universe described by James in *Essays in Radical Empiricism* and *A Pluralistic Universe*—one where we are called on to be participants.

James urges us to respond to this invitation, to rise to the occasion, to draw on energies heretofore latent. He urges us to act heroically. Heroes are usually described in terms of their exhibition of courage, and courage is often described in terms of an individual's ability to face death and dying. If this is so, if James's texts call on us to act heroically, to exercise the will to believe in the face of death, we might say that what James is about in these and other texts is showing us how to face death.

But the issue is a complicated one because this image does not appear instantly on the stage. Differently stated, James's texts have both a "latent" and a "manifest" image. Manifestly, they offer us detailed descriptions of the self, nature, and the interactions required from both. These descriptions are themselves radical and innovative; the self is described as a process, consciousness as a stream, nature as a "concatenated" flux, receiving its final touches from our hands.

But James's descriptions eventually disclose the impossibility of any complete description. His texts turn out to be "directive" rather than "descriptive" in nature, pointing beyond themselves back into experience. His texts are partial and unfinished interpretations rather than neutral observations. The latent image they present holds that no complete description is possible and, further, even if offered, would be rejected.

The latent content does indeed call on us to bear a heavy burden, to give up the security of certainty, to act heroically by embracing the finitude of our remarks. In this sense, his texts offer a way of dealing with death, that is, finitude, difficult and demanding as that may be.

# Acknowledgments

For over four decades, I have had the opportunity to teach courses on American philosophy and William James in particular at the University of Southern Maine. I am most grateful for all the insights provided by USM students during this period of time.

Ms. Kaye Kunz, my work-study student, did a wonderful job of organizing a first draft of this manuscript.

My wife Cathy spent endless hours organizing, typing, and proofreading this text. This book is dedicated to her.

Ms. Dee Mortensen, senior sponsoring editor at Indiana University Press, provided constant support and enthusiasm for this project, as well as displaying generous patience in awaiting its conclusion.

John Stuhr has from the outset been a persistent advocate for this book.

I am most grateful to the following publishers for permission to use material already published in whole or in part:

*William James Studies* for permission to use "'Problem' vs. 'Trouble': James, Kafka, Dostoevsky, and 'The Will to Believe'" (vol. 2, no. 1, 2007).

Indiana University Press for permission to use "Pragmatism and Death: Method vs. Metaphor, Tragedy vs. the Will to Believe," which appeared in *100 Years of Pragmatism: William James's Revolutionary Philosophy,* edited by John J. Stuhr (Indiana University Press, 2010).

# Abbreviations

Citations of the writings of William James are included in an abbreviated format in all chapters for ease of reference. All abbreviated citations and references are to *The Works of William James,* published by Harvard University Press (Frederick Burkhardt, general editor, and Fredson Bowers, textual editor). The abbreviations and full references (including original publication dates) are as follows:

ECR     *Essays, Comments, and Reviews* (1987 [1865–1909])
EP     *Essays in Philosophy* (1978 [1876–1910])
ERE     *Essays in Radical Empiricism* (1976 [1912])
ERM     *Essays in Religion and Morality* (1982 [1884–1910])
MEN     *Manuscript Essays and Notes* (1988 [1872–1910])
MT     *The Meaning of Truth* (1975 [1909])
Prag     *Pragmatism: A New Name for Some Old Ways of Thinking* (1975 [1907])
PP     *The Principles of Psychology* (1981 [1890]: 2 vols.)
PU     *A Pluralistic Universe* (1977 [1909])
SPP     *Some Problems of Philosophy* (1979 [1910])
TT     *Talks to Teachers on Psychology* (1983 [1899])
VRE     *The Varieties of Religious Experience* (1985 [1902])
WB     *The Will to Believe and Other Essays in Popular Philosophy* (1979 [1897])

# William James
# in Focus

# 1

# James's Life

*Will to Believe as Affirmation*

William James was born on January 11, 1842, in New York City, at the Astor House.[1] His father's father made a great deal of money. Among other things, he invested in the Erie Canal. At one time, he was reputed to be the second-richest person in New York State, after John Jacob Astor. James's father inherited a considerable amount of this fortune; he also suffered a serious accident, which required that his leg be amputated at the knee. This loss of mobility gave him large amounts of time to dote on the education of his children, the two most famous of whom were William and Henry, although Alice was a formidable figure in her own right. William made the first of many trips to Europe at the age of two. In the 1850s, he attended a private school in New York City, where he impressed his drawing teacher with his natural talent for sketching. During the period 1855–58, he was in London and Paris and attended college in Boulogne-sur-Mer; in 1859, he was at school in Newport, Rhode Island. In 1860, he was at the Academy in Geneva. In 1861, he was back in America, studying painting under William Hunt. James's father, however, did not approve of art as a vocation. A devotee of Emanuel Swedenborg, he believed that salvation could only be granted en masse, *not* through individual effort. This was something William could never accept.

From 1864 until 1869, James attended Harvard Medical School, receiving an MD in the last year of this period. This was the only degree James received, but he never did practice. This in itself was truly remarkable when we remember that James is often called "the father of American psychology" and that he, together with Charles Sanders Peirce and John Dewey, is considered to be one of the three founding fathers of the philosophy known as pragmatism. James was, in short, a true interdisciplinarian—far ahead of his time.

From 1865 to 1866, James accompanied Louis Agassiz to Brazil on an expedition dedicated to refuting the newly formulated theories of Charles Darwin. For James, the expedition was not successful; he came down with varioloid, a form of smallpox, strong enough to put him in the hospital. He did, however, become quite infatuated with the wildness of Brazil and its native power. This may have had an effect on his later concept of "pure experience."

From 1868 to 1870, James went through a period of extreme depression—something that we will return to shortly. He did, however, manage to overcome it. Subsequently, President Charles William Eliot of Harvard offered him a teaching job, and, in the 1873–74 school year, he became an instructor in anatomy, physiology, and natural history. He taught his first course in psychology in 1875. William married Alice Howe Gibbens in 1878; that same year, he signed a contract to write a psychology text. It was supposed to take two years to complete; instead, it took twelve years. The amount of time James took to write the book greatly frustrated his publisher, but the end result made James internationally famous. During this time also, "The Sentiment of Rationality" was published (1879), and James taught his first course in philosophy (1879). He bought a summer home in Chocorua, New Hampshire, in 1886, reputedly because it had fourteen doors, all opening "outward." His sister Alice coyly commented that his mind was not limited to only fourteen! James's writing became more prolific after *The Principles of Psychology (PP)*. *The Will to Believe and Other Essays in Popular Philosophy (WB)* was published in 1897, and *Talks to Teachers on Psychology and to Students on Some of Life's Ideals (TT)* in 1899. During the period 1901–1902, James gave the prestigious Gifford Lectures at Edinburgh University. These were subsequently published as *The Varieties of Religious Experience (VRE)*. The lectures, subsequently published as *Pragmatism: A New Name for Some Old Ways of Thinking (Prag)*, were delivered at the Lowell Institute in Boston in November and December of 1906.

That same year, James resigned from Harvard at almost fifty-six years of age. He had been trying to do so for some time, but pressure from the university president forced him to remain longer than he wished. James gave the Hibbert Lectures on Pluralism at Oxford University in 1908. These were published in 1909, as was the text titled *The Meaning of Truth (MT)*. From March to August, James was in Europe, where he had frequently journeyed for health issues during his lifetime. He returned to America in August 1910, seeming almost to "hold on" until he made it back to his summer home in Chocorua. *Essays in Radical Empiricism (ERE)*, a series of papers for which James had drawn up a rough table of contents, was published posthumously in 1912.

So much for the highpoints of James's life; these constitute the "manifest image," so to speak. That manifest image has as its central apex James's conflict with nihilism, depression, and death. Let us see how this came about.

As is clear from the above, for the first three decades or so of his life, James led a unique, somewhat pampered, and rather unusual lifestyle. He was placed in and removed from several educational contexts, turned to painting, gave that up for a career in science, ultimately completing something else again, namely, an MD degree. Moreover, James's health at this time was not robust; he lost the use of his eyesight twice, suffered from insomnia and weakness of the back, and had gastrointestinal disturbances and periodic exhaustion. Moreover, his afflictions were also of a psychological nature, leading to deep depression and to a feeling that his will was inefficacious and paralyzed. He had several times gone to Europe for the "sulphur baths" for his various illnesses. James writes to his father from Berlin on September 5, 1867: "Although I cannot exactly say that I got low-spirited, yet thoughts of the pistol, the dagger, and the bowl began to usurp an unduly large part of my attention, and I began to think that some change, even if a hazardous one was necessary."[2] This personal conflict with nihilism and subsequent temptation to commit suicide continued into 1870, when James writes in his diary,

> Today I about touched rock bottom, and perceive plainly that I must
> face the choice with open eyes: shall I frankly throw the moral busi-
> ness overboard, as one unsuited to my innate aptitudes, or shall I fol-
> low it and it alone, making everything else merely stuff for it?[3]

The "moral business" referred to here is that of a meaningful life, specifically the question of whether one can act efficaciously in pursuing chosen goals. By April 30 of that year, 1870, a definite change had come over James, through reading the works of the French philosopher Charles Renouvier. He writes in a notebook,

> I think that yesterday was a crisis in my life. I finished the first part of Renouvier's
> second "Essais" and see no reason why his definition of Free Will—the sustaining of
> a thought because I choose to when I might have other thoughts—need be the defi-
> nition of an illusion. . . . My first act of free will will be to believe in free will . . . Not
> in maxims, not in *Anschauungen* [contemplative views], but in accumulated acts of
> thought lies salvation. . . . Hitherto, when I have felt like taking a free initiative like
> daring to act originally, without carefully waiting for contemplation of the external
> world to determine all for me suicide seemed the most manly form to put my daring
> into; now, I will go a step further with my will, not only act with it, but believe as
> well; believe in my individual reality and creative power. My belief, to be sure, can't
> be optimistic—but I will posit life (the real, the good) in the self-governing resistance
> of the ego to the world. Life shall [be built in] doing and suffering and creating.[4]

In addition to this manifest image of James's personal life, there is also a sub-text, a "latent image," if you will. This latent image has three aspects: the realization that this issue of freedom versus determinism cannot be solved as a seeming "problem" or quadratic equation but is one rather of "affirming" a position; second, the realization that this affirmation is not a once-and-for-all-time decision but must be reaffirmed continually; and, third, the realization that this task, because it will remain eternally unfinished, is a difficult one for James to carry out. Or differently stated, for James, writing the text throughout his life span is exercising "the will to believe." We return to this point in the epilogue.

## Solving versus Affirming

What James realized in this instance is that what we might abstractly term the philosophical problem of freedom versus determinism cannot be solved on exclusively logical grounds or by an appeal to neutral empirical data. That is, one could construct a coherent argument for determinism—that we are the victims of our circumstances—and bolster it by showing that it corresponded to data—in this case, primarily the data of James's physical disorders and of his lack of any gainful employment thus far. On the other hand, one could construct an argument that the human self is free and able to act creatively and efficaciously; this argument, too, could be bolstered by appeal to corresponding empirical data—in this case, for example, by referring to James's successful pursuit of a medical degree. But when all is said and done, the arguments are inconclusive or indeterminate. Two competing hypotheses of equal worth can be put forth, both passing the traditional criteria of logical coherence and confirmation through correspondence with empirical facts. In brief, what James realized on a personal level in 1870 was that, first, the issue of freedom versus determinism was ambiguous or "vague" and, second, that this vagueness was what was most important about it. The problem cannot be solved but only be "resolved" through affirmation or action. For, in a vague situation like this, one is forced to react, and this participation is at least sometimes constitutive of the outcome. The issue of his own freedom versus determinism was richer, subtler than what appeared at the manifest level in terms of linguistic or conceptual categories.

## Sustained or Continual Affirmation

The action taken by James in 1870 was not a onetime affair. There were other crises in James's life that called for a similar type of response. Other commentators have unveiled different crises in James's life. Thus, Daniel Bjork, in *William James: The Center of his Vision,* views the period between 1899 and 1902 as a time when James suffered a deep depression "perhaps even more severe" than the melancholia of 1869.[5] James irreparably strained his heart while walking in the mountains of Keene Valley, New York, in 1898. For Bjork, James tried to deal with this second crisis in the same way as he did the first one, that is, by choosing an attitude, by redirecting and refocusing his vision: "Yet what worked in 1870 was not so workable in 1900. The active will was more likely to be broken during a terminal illness."[6]

Charlene Haddock Seigfried sees three crises in James's life; the first, the well-known 1867–70 encounter with nihilism; the second occurring in 1895, as James began more and more to realize that the descriptive positivism he advocated in *PP* (discussed below) was inadequate; and the third as occurring in the fifth chapter of *A Pluralistic Universe (PU).* In this chapter, one directly confessional, James renounces the ability of "intellectualist logic" to deal with reality.[7]

Comments such as these give rise to the suggestion that James's response to personal crises was of a continual nature rather than a onetime occurrence, that is, that a position in a vague situation must not only be taken but also continually reaffirmed. Such reaffirmation will not always be equally successful, reminding us possibly that we are "human, all too human," that is, fallible and vulnerable to failure.

This last point made serves as a reminder that doing philosophy for James required some effort. As he returned from the Agassiz expedition to Brazil, he wrote to his brother: "When I get home, I'm going to study philosophy all my days."[8] Yet he does not do so. He accepts a job, offered by Eliot, the president of Harvard, to teach physiology and astronomy. He decided to do so reluctantly, saying that the "decision seems 'the wiser if the tamer than the other and nobler lot in life,'" which was to work at philosophy independently as his father had done. Philosophy, he thought, "as a *business* is not normal for most men, and not for me. To be responsible for a complete conception of things is beyond my strength."[9] Cushing Strout notes that James had indicated an early interest in philosophy but repressed it for some time:

> At the age of fifty-seven James was at last prepared, with some trepidation, to give his full attention to those philosophical issues which had defined his ambition at the age of twenty-three. Suffering from a valvular lesion of the heart, four years after his resignation [from Harvard] he died, convinced that his philosophy was "too much like an arch built only on one side." Nearly all his professional work . . . began when he thought his professional career was finished.[10]

Strout's astute analysis suggests that writing the text was for James a continual affirmation and reaffirmation of the will to believe. As Strout notes,

> The elder James believed that men fell from grace individually, but could be saved collectively in a redeemed socialized society. His son, however, needed an individual salvation not only through faith but also in works. To translate this theological idiom, he needed to believe that there was a point and purpose to some particular work of his own with social meaning. *He would finally save himself through his writing.*[11]

Reading the text in this manner allows us the possibility of seeing things "from the point of view of the other." It is what James thought we should do, as expressed in "On a Certain Blindness in Human Beings": "The spectator's judgment is sure to miss the root of the matter and to possess no truth."[12] He gives as an example the instance of coming upon a number of farmed "coves" in North Carolina and viewing them as instances of squalor, but then realizing that, from the point of view of the meager planters, each of these coves "was a personal victory."[13] Analogously, James once said that "philosophic study means the habit of always seeing an alternative, of not taking the usual for granted, of making conventionalities fluid again, of imagining foreign states of mind."[14] Here we attempt to do something similar, that is, to view things from the point of view of the "other": in this case, James himself, to read his life and writings empathetically and not just descriptively.

James's conflict with nihilism and depression discloses a latent dimension to his thought—a continual preoccupation with death as an important topic. For example, in her recent biography of William James, titled *Genuine Reality*, Linda Simon tells us that

> As he wrote the Gifford lectures [in 1901], James, by his own admission, was obsessed with death: his own, certainly and during the year, four men he knew and esteemed. In January, Frederic Myers succumbed with James at his bedside. In March, James learned from Hugo Munsterberg that Leon Mendez Solomons, a former student of his who had been teaching at the University of Nebraska, was dead at the age of twenty-seven, following an appendectomy. In August, British physical researcher Henry Sidgwick died of cancer; in September, his beloved friend Thomas Davidson. James thought he himself might be dead soon too, before he realized his full potential.[15]

Indeed, in his own notes for his lectures for the *VRE*, James wrote,

> I find myself in a cold, pinched, quaking state . . . when I think of the probability of dying soon with all my music in me. My eyes are dry and hollow. My

facial muscles . . . won't contract, my throat quivers, my heart flutters, my
breast and body feel as if stale and caked. . . . I have forgotten, really *forgotten*, that mass of the world's joyous facts which in my healthful days filled me
with exultation about life. . . . The increasing pain and misery of more fully
developed disease—the disgust, the final strangulation etc., begin to haunt
me, I fear them; and the more I fear them, the more I think about them.[16]

Just as he wanted to give up teaching, so too did he want to give up the popular
style of lecturing for which he had become so famous and instead to write something serious and systematic—something that would bring "closure" to the process of describing life. Or so it seems, at first glance.

But the issue is a complicated one. On August 22, 1903, James had written to
Sarah Whitman,

I am convinced that the desire to formulate truths is a virulent disease. It has con-
tracted an alliance lately in me with a feverish personal ambition, which I never
had before, and which I recognize as an unholy thing in such a connection. I
actually dread to die until I have settled the Universe's hash in one more book.[17]

But, having admitted to this temptation, James goes on to chastise himself for
even entertaining such a consideration. He says (to himself), "Childish idiot—as
if the formulas about the Universe could ruffle its majesty and as if the common
sense world and its duties were not eternally the really real."[18] In his work *The
Wounded Storyteller: Body, Illness and Ethics*, Arthur Frank tells us "James feared his
ambition to settle 'the Universe's hash.' To settle the universe's hash is to place
oneself outside the vulnerability and contingency that being in the Universe involves. The intellectual infected with such an ambition ceases to think of himself as a body, thus disclaiming the vulnerability that bodies share."[19] Most importantly, for Frank, "Responsibility [individual responsibility] begins and ends with
the body."[20]

On November 6, 1909, the year before his death, James wrote to Henry Bow-
ditch, "I don't think *death* ought to have any terrors for one who has a positive life-record behind him, and when one's mind has once given up the *claim*
on life (which is kept up mainly by one's vanity, I think) the prospect of death is
gentle. . . . The great thing is to live *in* the passing day, and not look farther!"[21] But
his biographer Linda Simon charges that "James had not relinquished his claim on
life, had not completed his 'life-record,' and never had learned to live in the passing day. If death held no terror for him, its prospect filled him with regret."[22]

What are we to make of this? James himself wrote no treatise on death; indeed, that topic has only recently become an independent and fashionable one.

Nonetheless, the quotes mentioned above provide strong prima facie evidence that the issue was an important one for him. Can we, then, tease out the Jamesian attitude toward death? I think we can and that it would contain the following elements.

First, if James could have written the final book, the systematic or rigorous one, he perhaps would have attained an attitude of acceptance toward death. He would, perhaps, have "accepted the acceptance model" advocated by Dr. Elisabeth Kübler-Ross.[23] By writing such a book, James could have achieved some sort of relative immortality (something he seemed to long for, unsuccessfully, in religion) and, hence, could accept death—since it would not really *be* death. But we know that, factually, this did not occur. James's last book, the supposedly systematic one, turned out to be an introductory text, namely, *Some Problems of Philosophy (SPP)*. It was published some nine months after his death. Here, too, the text remains unfinished. "Say it is fragmentary and unrevised," James says. "Call it: 'A beginning of an introduction to Philosophy.' Say that I hoped by it to round my system, which now is too much like an arch built only on one side."[24]

The last thing James published during his lifetime was "A Pluralistic Mystic," a piece on Benjamin Paul Blood. It ends with James quoting approvingly Blood's statement: "'There is no conclusion. What has concluded, that we might conclude in regard to it? There are no fortunes to be told, and there is no advice to be given—Farewell.'"[25] Here, it seems, James did not write the final text and, hence, did not achieve acceptance. But I want to argue that James not only did not write the final text but that he *could* not do so, that is, for him, no text was final, in the sense of being able to capture life fully. Any final text would have been "disembodied," so to speak. James's texts, in short, remained unfinished and fragile; they remained a part of his body. The temptation to assume otherwise may have existed, as we shall see in the epilogue, but it needed to be resisted.

This "unfinishedness" being the case, the process would seem to be as important, or more important, than the product. James, then, would be on the side of those suggesting that we have been overly concerned with the "thing" death—as opposed to the process of dying. That is, we have been too concerned to reclaim certainty in a domain wherein vagueness dominates and where a healthy pluralism is necessary.

In both *PP* and *ERE,* James makes a plea for "thick" as opposed to "thin" descriptions of experience. *PU* ends with James saying that *"it is high time for the basis of discussion in these questions to be broadened and thickened up."*[26] This "thickness" might include the following: First, thickness demands that one emphasizes the transitions as much as the substances, the flights as well as the perchings, the relations as much as the terms that they connect. Second, among these relational phases, we must be sure to emphasize equally both the disjunctive and the conjunctive transitions. A decision to emphasize only the conjunctive transitions results in a Parmenidean or Hegelian outlook—which James disparagingly termed a "block universe." On the other hand, a decision to emphasize only the disjunctive transitions results in an "inhuman" universe wherein the self is reduced to a bundle of relations and where, in short, there is no self to refuse to "go gentle into that good night."

While admitting and, indeed, affirming the inevitable reality of the temporal and the finite throughout his career, James also said, "If this life be not a real fight in which something is eternally gained for the universe by success, it is no better than a game of private theatricals from which we may withdraw at will. It *feels* like a fight."[27] And again, in *Prag,* he says, "I find myself willing to take the universe to be really dangerous, without therefore backing out and crying 'no play'."[28]

In sum, we can find in James both elements of acceptance and elements of rebellion or denial regarding death and the process of dying. He seems both to have tried to reconcile himself to death by emphasizing past achievements and by living in the present and, hypothetically, by hinting that, if he could only write the final book, he would be able to reach acceptance. But there is part of him that continues to emphasize the personal, or the temporal, and the bodily. This part continues to reject death, even while acknowledging its inevitability. For James, the writing of the text was his act of rebellion or his exercising of "the will to believe." But the product thus produced always undermines itself through James's constant reminder to himself, and to us, that no text is final, that is, complete. All are, like the body, temporal.

James's own personal experience of depression and near suicide from 1868 to 1870 is verbalized and justified some twenty-six years later in the essay titled "The Will to Believe," although it has some precedent in an earlier essay titled "The Sentiment of Rationality." We now turn to these two pivotal essays in James's thought.

# 2

# "The Will to Believe"

*Policing versus Free-Roaming*

## The Sentiment of Rationality

In 1879 and 1882, James published two parts of articles that collectively would become known as "The Sentiment of Rationality." It is remarkable how much this early text anticipates his more mature and even his final positions in philosophy. He begins by looking over various conceptualizations of the universe and noting that, while some people seek out similarities, others seek out differences in providing descriptions. This became the notorious issue of "the one and the many," which James later called the most important problem in philosophy. Here he quickly moves on, telling the reader that "the only possible philosophy must be a compromise between an abstract monotony and a concrete heterogeneity."[1] But he quickly concluded from this that pluralism is necessary, that "none of our explanations are complete." A completed explanation is always perspectival and also incomplete. "In a word, so far as A and B contain $l,m,n$, and $o,p,q$ respectively, in addition to $x$, they are not explained by $x$. . . . A single explanation of a fact only explains it from a single point of view" (*WB*, 60). Going further, conceptualizations are teleological in nature. We see things from a particular point of view for a particular purpose. Hence, certainty is not possible.

But neither is it desirable. Suppose, he says, the goal of certainty was attained. "Our mind is so wedded to the process of seeing an *other* beside every item of its experience, that when the notion of an absolute datum is presented to it, it goes through its usual procedure and remains pointing at the void beyond . . ." (*WB*, 63). James terms this "ontological wonder-sickness" (ibid.), a disease for which there is no cure, or for which the "cure" is worse than the disease itself. When all is said and done, "the notion of a possible other than the actual may still haunt our imagination and prey upon our system. The bottom of being is logically opaque to us" (ibid., 64). Furthermore, this situation will never be solved or done away with. "Every generation will produce its Job, its Hamlet, its Faust." The world is "over-determined," to use Freud's term in a different context, and "there is nothing improbable in the supposition that an analysis of the world may yield a number of formulae, all consistent with the facts" (ibid., 66).

Given that we cannot logically "solve" the issue of which conceptualization of the universe is correct, what do we do? For we must, James claims, do *something*. We pick, James claims, one conception of the universe over the others for "sentimental" reasons. It is not a matter of rejecting logic and empirical data but rather of what to do *after* these have been used. James claims that there are two types of theories that we will not accept—for sentimental reasons. We will not accept a completely pessimistic theory, and we will not accept an outlook that does not give us at least a small role to play in life:

> A philosophy may be unimpeachable in other respects but either of two defects will be fatal to its universal acceptance. First, its ultimate principle must not be one that essentially baffles and disappoints our dearest desires and most cherished powers. . . . But a second and worse defect in a philosophy than that of contradicting our active propensities is to give them no object whatever to press against. Better face the enemy than the eternal void! (*WB*, 70–71)

James argues forcefully for this position, but there is no way that he can "prove" it completely. Indeed, given the title of the essay, calling for or assuming the attainment of such proof would constitute a contradiction in terms. Rather, one must have "faith" in one paradigm or outlook over the others: "Faith means belief in something concerning which doubt is still theoretically possible; and as the test of belief is willingness to act, one may say that faith is the readiness to act in a cause the prosperous issue of which is not certified to us in advance" (*WB*, 76).

Faith, then, involves risk; it is akin to moral courage, as in facing death; it lends itself to living life intensely. Furthermore, it is intergenerational, and the outcome will not be known until the last person has had her say. Struggle as we may, we are caught in a situation where "the only escape from faith is mental nullity" (*WB*, 78). In other words, consciousness requires commitment. Without faith we are "things," *en soi* in Jean-Paul Sartre's sense of the term. When we select one outlook over another, then, "Intellect, will, taste, and passion cooperate" (ibid., 77). Finally, there are some cases where faith creates its own verification. The example James uses is the same as that employed some years later in the article titled "The Will to Believe": "Suppose . . . that I am climbing in the Alps, and have the ill-luck to work myself into a position from which the only escape is by a terrible leap" (ibid., 80). In this case, James says, what one believes is partly constitutive of the outcome; furthermore, this example "is one of an immense class" (ibid., 76). In short, the proof of the pudding is in the leaping—though there are constraints to be placed on the purported leap. I can leap a six-foot gorge—perhaps. I cannot leap across the Grand Canyon. At first glance, this article might be taken to apply only to tender-minded domains, that is, matters of personal morals or relations with others. Or religion, as we shall see below. This might be termed its "manifest content." Such damage control would indeed keep James from going off the deep end of "accepted" philosophical discourse—but it does so at a price. It deradicalizes James and preserves the subject-object dichotomy as constituted by two different domains. Furthermore, it goes specifically against parts of the text where James accuses scientific thinkers of selecting a paradigm for "sentimental" reasons: "The necessity of faith as an ingredient in our mental attitude is strongly insisted on by the scientific philosophers of the present day; but by a singularly arbitrary caprice they say it is only legitimate when used in the interests of one particular proposition—the proposition, namely that the course of nature is uniform" (ibid.).

In an almost "Kuhnian" fashion,[2] James draws out similarities between science and religion, showing that belief is an operative factor in each domain, that science is not simply "open" and religion "closed." As James says, "The rules of the scientific game, burdens of proof, presumptions, *experimenta cruces*, complete inductions, and the like are only binding on those who enter that game" (*WB*, 78). Going further, he specifically uses an example from science to verify his position in this article, for example, in evolution, saving the present generation and ignoring the rest or helping the future generation at the expense of the present.

In short, the conservative way to take this piece would be to divide and conquer, to separate the tough minded and the tender minded, to have two domains and keep them well "policed." This strategy would have to ignore or repress the fact that James uses examples from science to make his point. Second, it would have to ignore or downplay the fact that James later offers "pragmatism" as a way to achieve a "marriage" between the tough minded and the tender minded. This attempt to curtail the use of the sentimental might be viewed as a form of repression. It would also preserve a view of philosophy as analytic, objective, and logical in nature. Conversely, a blurring of the lines between the rational and the sentimental might ultimately result in a redefinition of philosophy, offering a more "intimate" and "down-to-earth" experience.

## The Will to Believe

In "The Will to Believe," James defends each person's right to choose that hypothesis which is most appealing in a situation where the options are "living," "forced," and "momentous." A "live option" is one between two living hypotheses, "living" being defined as existing as a real possibility for the person to whom it is proposed. A "dead" option is one that does not make any sense or constitute any appeal.[3] Hence, the question "Whose outlook do you prefer, Skovoroda's or Philo Judaeus's?" is a live option for only a very small number of people. Going further, the situation must be forced *and* living *and* momentous. A situation that contains one, or even two, of these characteristics is not one where the will to believe is applicable. A situation could be live, momentous, but not forced; or live, forced, but not momentous, etc. However, when the three characteristics are present, we have the "right" to choose one option over the other for passionate or sentimental reasons. Logic and empirical data have not been rejected; they have, rather, been exhausted, leaving only "sentiment":

> Our passional nature not only lawfully may, but must, decide an option between propositions, whenever it is a genuine option that cannot by its nature be decided on intellectual grounds; for to say, under such circumstances, "Do not decide, but leave the question open," is itself a passional decision—just like deciding yes or no—and is attended with the same risk of losing the truth. (WB, 20)

What is not clear is just how many live options there are and how one goes about distinguishing such situations from others. On the one hand, as in "The Sentiment of Rationality," James is careful here to assert, first, that certainty is not a possibility: "Objective evidence and certitude are doubtless very fine ideals to play with, but where on this moonlit and dream-visited planet are they found?" (WB, 22). And again: "I live, to be sure, by the practical faith that we must go on experiencing and thinking over our experience, for only thus can our opinions grow more true; but to hold any one of them—*I absolutely do not care which*—as if it never could be reinterpretable or corrigible, I believe to be a tremendously mistaken attitude" (ibid.).

On the other hand, even granted that there is no certainty, James is still careful to assert that one cannot simply make something true by believing in it. For example, we cannot just believe that we are well while lying in bed overpowered by rheumatism; we cannot feel sure that the two dollars in our pocket are one hundred dollars, etc. The reason for this is that the will to believe is only operative in those situations wherein one has two diverse hypotheses, each equally coherent and each capable of corresponding to empirical data to an equal extent. But here a further problem arises, for James himself at times seems to demarcate the area of science from that of religion/morals—in terms of where the will to believe applies. He says, "in our dealings with objective nature we obviously are recorders, not makers, of the truth; and decisions for the mere sake of deciding promptly and getting on to the next business would be wholly out of place. Throughout the breadth of physical nature facts are what they are quite independently of us" (*WB*, 26). Such a demarcation, while apparently simple and acceptable, represents a preservation of the status quo, that is, the subject-object dichotomy. It must be admitted that James himself is responsible for some of the confusion here. On the one hand, he at times sets up the criteria of forced, living, and momentous decisions and seems at least to leave the door open to scientific hypothesis to enter into this domain. From such a perspective, science qua science would not be excluded, but only those sets of hypotheses that were either not forced or not living or not momentous. On the other hand, he sometimes speaks as if our scientific hypotheses were, by definition, inaccessible to the will to believe: "The questions here [in science] are always trivial questions, the hypotheses are hardly living (at any rate not living for us spectators), the choice between believing truth or falsehood is seldom forced" (ibid.).

In seeming opposition to this scientific domain, where the will to believe is not applicable, are three areas where it is applicable. These include questions that focus on morals, interpersonal relationships, and religion. The question, then, is whether the will to believe is limited to these latter domains and perhaps similar ones or whether it should be recognized elsewhere. I suggest that James is at his best when he distinguishes forced, living, and momentous situations from nonforced, living, momentous situations, letting the philosophical chips fall where they may. There are no hypotheses that, by domain of definition or content, are excluded from the will to believe. The "manifest content" of the will to believe may seem domain-specific, that is, applying only to "soft" disciplines. However, the "latent content" of the will to believe discloses that there is no area from which it is denied admission.

This second, latent view does have additional metaphysical presuppositions. The will to believe does not stand alone; it has a context. It makes sense only in an unfinished universe, one where personal preference may sometimes become a constituting aspect of the outcome. As the French philosopher Gabriel Marcel once said, "Being is, as it were, attested."[4] In other words, being is not a problem to be solved, but rather something we are involved with rather than looking at. We must resist the temptation to see being or reality as a problem and then attempt to solve it. We can locate ourselves within the mysterious situation, but we cannot, or should not, turn the mystery into a problem, in Marcel's terms. Ellen Suckiel has caught some of the flavor of this when she suggests that the last step of James's faith ladder, a clone of the will to believe, "may be considered not as a descriptive claim about God, but rather as a performative utterance by which the subject takes the leap and both attains and proclaims a religious commitment."[5] Hilary Putnam has argued that the will to believe is akin to that situation faced by Pierre in Sartre's "Existentialism and Humanism." This is not, in other words, a mere matter of calculating the consequences and then choosing on this basis. This is not something the scientific method can help you with, even if, as Putnam notes, "your conception of the scientific method is as generous as Dewey's."[6] We also fail to notice, Putnam argues, "that [the will to believe] is meant to apply to the individual's choice of a philosophy, including pragmatism itself." Furthermore, the need to believe "in advance of evidence" is, Putnam argues, not domain-specific, that is, not policed: "It plays an essential role in science itself."[7] Putnam tells us that James's claim—which "paradoxically the logical positivists helped to make part of conventional philosophy of science with their distinction between the context of discovery and the context of justification—was that science could not progress if we insisted that scientists never believe or defend theories except on sufficient evidence."[8] The difference between science and religion seems to be one of degree rather than one of kind, at least on this matter.

In sum, "The Will to Believe" appears on the surface to be dealing exclusively with clearly marked-out domains or areas, namely, morality, interpersonal relationships, and religion. This is its "manifest image." The latent image of the will to believe suggests that there are no areas to which it is forbidden access, only the requirement that the option be forced, living, and momentous. Furthermore, the latent content also suggests that the will to believe is not a "problem" to be solved, in Deweyan terminology.[9] Rather it is to be viewed as a stance or posture toward the universe, an admission and affirmation that the universe is "wild, game flavored as a hawk's wing." Third, this latent content suggests that this affirmation is not a onetime affair, but rather a stance that we must continually reaffirm, with varying degrees of success. The poignancy of this last revelation may pose the question "Does this ask too much of us?" James would probably answer, "We won't know until we try." As he put it at the end of the article, quoting Fitz-James Stephen,

> In all important transactions of life we have to take a leap in the dark. . . . If a man chooses to turn his back altogether on God and the future, no one can prevent him. No one can show beyond reasonable doubt that he is mistaken. If a man thinks otherwise and acts as he thinks, I do not see that any one can prove that he is mistaken. Each must act as he thinks best; and if he is wrong, so much the worse for him. We stand on a mountain pass in the midst of whirling snow and blinding mist, through which we get glimpses now and then of paths which may be deceptive. If we take the wrong road we shall be dashed to pieces. We do not certainly know whether there is any right one. What must we do? "Be strong and of a good courage." Act for the best, hope for the best, and take what comes. . . . if death ends all, we cannot meet death better. (*WB*, 33)

The pervasiveness of the "will to believe" in James's thought had as a precedent the realization that consciousness, previously viewed as a neutral object, was, in actuality, constitutive or shaping in the very act of awareness itself. This takes place in his famous text titled *The Principles of Psychology*. The manifest content of that text centers around the rejection of consciousness as a substance and its affirmation as a "stream." The latent content consists of the realization that consciousness, because it is constitutive in the very act of being aware, cannot be neutral or objective in character, but rather molds or shapes, like an artist, in the very act of knowing. It also consists in the realization and affirmation that psychology, initially described as an isolated, positivistic phenomenon, has metaphysical implications. Let us see how this comes about.

# 3

## *The Principles of Psychology*

### *Consciousness as a Constitutive Stream*

*The Principles of Psychology (PP),* James's first major work, was twelve years in the making and earned for him the title "father of American psychology." Initially, James adopted a "functional dualism" for this text, separating the domain of psychology from other domains, such as metaphysics: "Every natural science assumes certain data critically. . . . Psychology, the science of finite individual minds, assumes as its data (1) *thoughts and feelings,* and (2) *a physical world* with which they coexist and which (3) *they know.* Of course these data are discussible; but the discussion of them (as of other elements) is called metaphysics and falls outside the province of this book."[1] And again, "This book consequently rejects both the associational and the spiritualist theories; and in this strictly positivistic point of view consists the only feature of it for which I feel tempted to claim originality" (*PP,* 1: 6). This, then, is the "manifest image" presented by James to the reader. Also part of the manifest image is his radically new view of consciousness as a stream rather than an object or a substance. The latent content of his position becomes manifest when he realizes that the dualism he espouses cannot be maintained and that psychology leaks into metaphysics itself. This chapter focuses primarily on an analysis of the "stream of consciousness" and to the realization that its characteristics, as outlined by James, entail its undoing as a neutrally functioning object.

James identifies five characteristics of consciousness. The fact that he utilized only four characteristics when writing the shorter version of *PP* would seem to indicate that these divisions were overlapping rather than mutually exclusive. One way of grouping the divisions of the stream might be to say that the first, fourth, and fifth characteristics emphasize intensity or zest, while the second and third remind us that intensity is cumulative or that richness is a cocriterion. It is this division that we shall adopt here. According to James,

1. Every thought tends to be a part of a personal consciousness;
2. It [consciousness] always appears to deal with objects other than itself; that is, it is cognitive, or possesses the function of knowing;
3. It is interested in some parts of these objects to the exclusion of others, and welcomes or rejects—chooses among them. . . . all the while. (*PP,* 1: 220)

In calling all thoughts "personal," James immediately stresses involvement on the part of each of us. There are no impartial thoughts existing as transcendental spectators, impartially viewing the game of life. Every thought is "owned" or, better, "tends to appear" as owned, thus leaving space for the "facts of subconscious personality" or "*secondary personal selves*" (*PP,* 1: 222). James is here advocating the efficacy of consciousness. The reason is simple: consciousness must have a role to play if life is to be intense—a "real fight." Consciousness must be personally involved if we are to get from life that sense of zest that James was always seeking. At this stage, however, the only way James sees to uphold the active power of consciousness is to adopt a dualism. Indeed, there are several places in *PP* where he explicitly adopts a dualistic approach. For example,

*The psychologist's attitude toward cognition . . . is a thorough going dualism.*
It supposes two elements, mind knowing and thing known, and treats them as irreducible. Neither gets out of itself or into the other, neither in any way *is* the other, neither *makes* the other. (ibid., 1: 214)

The problem confronting James is clear: What approach to life will allow for the personal efficacy of consciousness and, hence, the intensity of experience? A dualistic approach would satisfy this demand but at the cost of bifurcating experience. By separating experience into two parts, dualism impoverishes the original richness of experience. While James himself is unclear here and continually rejects and then returns to dualism in *PP,* there are at least some signs of the discomfort he felt in adopting dualism. This is most readily seen in the analysis of the fourth and fifth characteristics of consciousness.

Consciousness, as cognitive, appears to deal with, or "intends," an object. Conception is defined by James as "neither the mental state nor what the mental state signifies, but the relation between the two, namely, the *function* of the mental state in signifying just that particular thing" (*PP,* 1: 436). Consciousness as portrayed here is bipolar. A division of experience into consciousness on one side and objectivity on the other is an inadequate abstraction. A richer view of consciousness than the one posited by dualism is needed. James realized that, in talking about experience, we may say either "atoms producing consciousness" or "consciousness produced by atoms." To say either atoms alone or consciousness alone is precisely equal mutilations of the truth.[2] James here is looking for a view of consciousness that will, at one and the same time, keep it active and continuous with the rest of experience. His initial step is to assert that a distinction must be made between the object of consciousness and the object in itself. Consciousness, as intention, is constitutive of the former of these. Furthermore, since consciousness is intentional at all times, the only object I am aware of in being conscious is the constituted object. Widespread failure on the part of psychologists to note the inadequacy of the division of experience into the categories "subjective" and "objective" has led to what James called the "psychologist's fallacy":

> The great snare of the psychologist is the confusion of his own standpoint with that of the *mental fact* about which he is making his report. . . . The Psychologist . . . stands outside the mental state he speaks of. Both itself and its object are objects for him. Now when it is a cognitive state (percept, thought, concept, etc.) he ordinarily has no other way of naming it than as the thought, percept, etc., *of that object*. He himself, meanwhile, knowing the self-same object in *his* way, gets easily led to suppose that the thought, which is *of* it, knows it in the same way in which he knows it, although this is often very far from being the case. (*PP*, 1: 195)

Though James himself is not as clear here as he could be, nonetheless, he seems to be moving toward the position that each thought, *including the psychologist's thought*, is constitutive of an object, and, therefore, no analysis of consciousness as dualistically divided into subjective and objective is correct. Hence, any awareness of reality can no longer be regarded as impartial because each and every awareness of experience is intentional, that is, constitutive. If this were so, all conscious experience would seem to be intense because we are forced to mold and shape, or "create," our objects. In all conscious experience, we are artists, selecting certain aspects to highlight and neglecting others. This point needs to be emphasized, because its implications extend far beyond *PP*. From a metatheoretical or self-reflective perspective, *PP* needs to be viewed as an interpretive text and not just as a descriptive one.[3]

It is the fifth characteristic of consciousness that emphasizes its being interested more in one part of its object than another, and its welcoming and rejecting or choosing all the while it thinks. The senses are nothing but selective organs that pick out, from among all the movements of experience, those that fall within certain limits of velocity. The barest perception possible is a focalization. We see *this* as opposed to *that,* here as opposed to *there,* etc.:

> Out of what is in itself an indistinguishable swarming continuum, devoid
> of distinction or emphasis, our senses make for us, by attending to this
> motion and ignoring that, a world full of contrasts, or sharp accents, of
> abrupt changes, of picturesque light and shade. (*PP,* 1: 274)

Two insights can be gleaned here. First of all, James is again emphasizing the active role of consciousness. Life is intense because by our choices we are creating it. "Things," from this point of view, are not separate impartial entities but rather, "special groups of sensible qualities, which happen practically or aesthetically to interest us, to which we therefore give substantive names, and which we exalt to [the] . . . exclusive status of independence and dignity" (ibid.).

On the other hand, it is only because the simplest sensation is richer than we have heretofore acknowledged that selection is possible. What we hear is not simply thunder but thunder-preceded-by-silence (*PP,* 1: 234). We shall return to this when discussing the second and third characteristics of consciousness. For the present, let us note simply that selectivity makes consciousness intense, but one must select *from* something. It is only because the present moment of consciousness is ongoing, has *more* to it than we have noticed, that selection can take place. Focalization, in brief, depends on a fringe. This fringe is the unfinished continuum from which we create ourselves by our selective choices.

Not only do sensations select (for example, a given velocity of sound waves to "hear"), but also, from the sensations we do have, we select some to call "true" and some to call "false." Thus, for example, I select the view of my table top as square and to be the "true" one, relegating other possibilities, such as two acute and two obtuse angles, to the status of "perspectival" (*PP,* 1: 274). In two senses, then, perception is selective. Reasoning proper is even more selective, consisting as it does in a choice of one aspect of an object as the "essence" and a subsuming of the object, now properly labeled, into its proper conceptual framework. Logically speaking, there are many such frameworks, and we simply select that one most suitable to our present needs. Consciousness, then, is selective at all levels:

> consciousness is at all times primarily *a selecting agency.* Whether we take it in
> the lowest sphere of sense, or in the highest of intellection, we find it always
> doing one thing, choosing one out of several of the materials so presented to
> its notice, emphasizing and accentuating that and suppressing as far as pos-
> sible all the rest. The item emphasized is always in close connection with some
> interest felt by consciousness to be paramount at the time. (*PP,* 1: 142)

We are always aware, then, in terms of our needs and interests. To be conscious at all is to be partial, or, in other terms, rationality is prescriptive. Life is intense because each of us is involved with its making. There is no possibility of being impartial or of arriving at objectivity. Jacques Barzun realized the connection between ambiguity and creativity in art, as the following quote indicates:

> [In *PP*] James struck a deathblow at Realism. The then prevailing views
> of the mind were that it copied reality like a photographic plate, that it re-
> ceived and assembled the elements of experience like a machine, that it com-
> bined ideas like a chemist. For this "scientist" mind, James substituted one that
> was a born artist—a wayward, creative mind impelled by inner wants, fringed
> with mystery, and capable of infinitely subtle, unrecordable nuances.[4]

But this is only half the story. A cursory reading of James's statements on selectivity might lead one to conclude that one can select capriciously anything one wants to be aware of and, further, that each of these selections has no relation to others. This is by no means the case. Selection is possible only because consciousness is an unfinished stream from which I am *continually* forced to choose. The choosing renders life intense, but each choosing, precisely because it is a moment in a cumulative process, cuts off alternatives for the future. In brief, James's defense of the efficacy of consciousness is part and parcel of his view that consciousness is richer than we have realized, that it has substantive and transitive parts, which overlap. These are discussed under the second and third characteristics of consciousness, namely that,

1. Within each personal consciousness thought is always changing, and
2. Within each personal consciousness thought is sensibly continuous.
   (*PP*, 1: 220)

The first of these two aspects asserts that change is a definite element in consciousness and must be dealt with as such. No single state of consciousness, once it has gone, can recur and be identical with what it was before. Something has occurred in between these two appearances; these interim occurrences cannot be ignored, save by arbitrary whim. At the very least, the *time* of the two appearances is different. Furthermore, the second of the two must take the first one into account, in terms of the present context. Each present state of consciousness, then, is partly determined by the nature of the entire past succession. As James says, "Experience is re-molding us every moment, and our mental reaction on every given thing is really a resultant of our experience of the whole world wound up to that date" (*PP*, 1: 228).

Here James clearly casts his vote with the reality of change. Each and every moment of consciousness is at least temporally different from any previous one. As temporally different, it must take into account different circumstances. Each succeeding present moment has one additional past moment to take in or appropriate and, therefore, cannot be taken as identical with it. What has happened, however, is that certain schools of thought, intrigued with finding factual certainty "beneath" this "apparent" process, have reduced this rich complexity to simplicity. Seizing on one aspect of an experience as basic and finding this aspect repeated in other experiences, these schools have "taken the part for the whole," ignored the temporal context of each moment of consciousness, and articulated a view of consciousness wherein all its variations are reduced to combinations of certain simple, basic elements. The second aspect of consciousness emphasizes the fact that experience is richer than we have admitted. It has contextual nuances that have to be taken into account; in particular, the temporal aspect of each moment of consciousness should not be repressed. Change is real; no thought can be had twice in the exact same manner. As James himself so forcefully puts it, *"A permanently existing 'idea' or 'Vorstellung' which makes its appearance before the footlights of consciousness at periodical intervals, is as mythological an entity as the Jack of Spades"* (*PP*, 1: 230).

Not only does consciousness change, but also the changing is an ongoing process. As an unfinished continuum, consciousness has both substantive and transitive parts. The transitions between two substantive moments of consciousness are as real as the substantive moments themselves. Conscious states, in other words, are continuous, because transitional fringes connect them. For example, James asks that we consider what a conscious awareness of thunder would be like: "Into the awareness of the thunder itself the awareness of the previous silence creeps and continues; for what we hear when the thunder crashes is not thunder *pure*, but thunder-breaking-upon-silence-and-contrasting-with-it" (*PP*, 1: 234).

These transitive elements are represented in language by such words as *of, and, but*, etc. These are all contrast words. We are aware of this *and not* that, this part *of* that, etc. Once again, we need to recall that consciousness, as selective, is forced to mold experience. On the other hand, the experience in and through which the molding takes place presents itself as a continuum, or in James's words, a stream: "Consciousness . . . does not appear to itself chopped up in bits. Such words as 'chain' or 'train' do not describe it fitly as it presents itself in the first instance. It is nothing jointed; it flows. A 'river' or a 'stream' are the metaphors by which it is most naturally described" (*PP*, 1: 233).

In each conscious experience, then, there is always a main substantive point, arrived at in accordance with our needs at the time and surrounded by a periphery of transitional aspects, that is, that this point chosen as substantive is *not* that, is *part* of this larger whole, is *like* that in one respect but not in another respect, etc. The point here is that each and every moment of consciousness is contextually articulated in terms of transitive elements and that these latter are part and parcel of conscious awareness. These transitive parts are relations; they are as real for James as the substantive parts that they relate: "If there be such things as feelings at all, then *so surely as relations between objects exist in* rerum natura, *so surely, and more surely, do feelings exist to which these relations are known*" (*PP,* 1: 238).

Conscious experience is richer than we have realized because it contains not only substantive elements, represented by nouns and adjectives, but also transitive elements, represented by disjunctions and conjunctions. These latter are both as real for conscious awareness as the substantive parts that they connect. They are found among the objects of the stream, which *is* a stream because it is composed, in a nonreductive manner, of interpenetrating substantive and transitive parts. Note that *both* the disjunctive and conjunctive transitions are equally real. A decision to recognize the ontological status of substantive parts and disjunctive parts would lead to the atomism of traditional empiricism. On the other hand, a decision to recognize the validity of substantive parts and the conjunctive transitions would tend to reject pluralism and, ultimately, to dismiss change as an illusion. James sees no reason for rejecting either transitive part. The result is a view of consciousness as a stream partially conjunctive and partially disjunctive.

Putting the second and third aspects together, then, we get a view of consciousness as a continuum, made up of substantive and transitive parts, yet also changing. Every image in conscious experience is

> steeped and dyed in the free water that flows round it. With it goes the
> sense of its relations, near and remote, the dying echo of whence it came
> to us, the dawning sense of whither it is to lead. . . . If I recite *a, b, c, d, e, f,*
> *g,* at the moment of my uttering *d* neither *a, b, c,* nor *e, f, g,* are out of my
> consciousness altogether, but both, after their respective fashions, "mix
> their dim lights" with the stronger one of the *d.* (*PP,* 1: 246–48)

Taken together, then, these two aspects of consciousness present us with a picture in "broad strokes" of an ongoing, unfinished continuum. Within this process, certain aspects are focused on and others remain on the fringe, or periphery, of consciousness. The most basic element of experience has duration here; it is a movement-going-into-the-past-and-a-new-tendency-toward-the-future. Each moment has a rearward- and forward-looking end. The present is no pinpoint or knife edge; rather, it should be viewed as a saddleback (*PP,* 1: 574), having a breath of its own. As Gerald Myers has noted,

> It was important, James believed, to realize that vagueness often characterizes our feelings and sensations; introspective psychology, to be accurate, must acknowledge this vagueness, and at the level of sensation and feeling—the "guts" of experience—vagueness is usually the harbinger of something further to be detected, the promise of a potential discovery.[5]

Here, for, example, is James's analysis of a sensation:

> A simple sensation . . . is an abstraction, and all our concrete states of mind are representations of objects with some amount of complexity. Part of the complexity is the echo of the objects just past, and in a less degree, perhaps, the foretaste of those just to arrive. Objects fade out of consciousness slowly. If the present thought is OF ABCDEFG, the next one will be of BCDEFGH, and the one after that of CDEFGHI—the lingerings of the past dropping successively away, and the incomings of the future making up the loss. These lingerings of old objects, these incomings of new, are the germs of memory and expectation, the retrospective and prospective sense of time. They give that continuity to consciousness without which it could not be called a stream. (*PP,* 1: 571–72)

Consciousness, in brief, is much richer than we have realized. It has much more than substantive parts, existing atomistically and awaiting the unifying idea of an outside agent. Rather are the relating transitions in consciousness to be taken into account; these are of both a disjunctive and conjunctive nature. Furthermore, consciousness is temporal, and the situational aspect of all thoughts, the fact that we can never have the same thought twice, can no longer be ignored. Note here that it is precisely because consciousness is an ongoing continuum, in which a simple sensation is impossible, that we have to be selective. Since the sensible present has duration and is characterized in terms of a coming-to-be-and-a-passing-away, we are always focusing on one part of it. Conscious experience is intense because we are forced to make decisions, to choose, to intend. But the selecting is a cumulative process. On the other hand, consciousness is far richer than we have noticed; it is unfinished and has interpenetrative, substantive, and transitive parts. As such, it causes us to be selective. In a word, the richness of consciousness demands its intensity, and vice versa. James himself found it difficult to articulate both of these notions with a single word. His closest attempt comes in the stream of consciousness chapter, where he says, "It is, in short, the reinstatement of the vague to its proper place in our mental life which I am anxious to press on the attention" (*PP,* 1: 246).

Conscious experience is vague, in the sense of being richer than any formula. It is unfinished and here also could be called vague. Finally, it is as *vague* that consciousness demands selectivity. In brief, experience, as an unfinished continuum, demands an intense life on the part of each of us; experience is infinitely rich in the sense of being still in the making, since the last person in experience has not had his or her say. The net result is the attempt to maintain as much of the richness at as intense a level as possible.

This then is the manifest image presented in *PP.* The very fact that it is described using an image, that is, a "stream," should give us pause for reflection. Metaphors reveal and conceal, simultaneously. James, as we shall note later, had a love-hate relationship with language, being able neither to live with it nor entirely without it. The description of consciousness as a stream, an ongoing focus/fringe continuum, is liberating. One can "return to life" enriched by its acquisition. But the description of consciousness as selective, and as intentional, discloses the fact that no portrayal is completely neutral. All are "interpretations"—rather than solely descriptive in nature. James himself at this stage does not indicate clearly how his own outlook, from a hermeneutical perspective, applies also to himself.

However, as early as 1893, in his article "The Knowing of Things Together," James begins to renounce his positivistic position and also his dualist portrayal of consciousness and objects as two different items of existence. He says, "I have become convinced since publishing that book [*PP*] that no conventional restrictions can keep metaphysical and so-called epistemological inquiries out of the psychology books."[6] In place of this James seeks out what exists prior to the division of experience into consciousness and content—what he will later term "pure experience." Here he tells the reader,

> Inside of the minimal pulse of experience which, taken as object, is change of feeling, and, taken as content, is feeling of change, is realized that absolute and essential self-transcendence which we swept away as an illusion when we sought it between a content taken as a whole and a supposed objective thing outside. *Here in the elementary datum of which both our physical and our mental worlds are built, we find both the original of presence in absence and the prototype of that operation of knowing many things together which it is our business to discuss.* (*EP,* 77)

For James, the smallest piece of experience takes time. The present moment is really the "passing moment" and can be counted twice over as both consciousness and as object. This becomes clearer in later texts, especially in *A Pluralistic Universe* and *Essays in Radical Empiricism*. There James develops his metaphysics of "pure experience" or "pluralistic pantheism." But first, an important preliminary theme must be looked at in his famous text *The Varieties of Religious Experience*. For it is there that the mystical experience is offered as perhaps the primary example or "exemplar" of pure experience. But, as we shall see, this theme, too, has both a latent and a manifest content. The seemingly descriptive account will give way to a more interpretive one, both revealing and concealing simultaneously. It will ultimately lead to the realization that a pure or complete description of experience is not possible and, once again, also not desirable.

# 4
# *The Varieties of Religious Experience*
### *Mysticism as a Vague "Exemplar"*

The very title *The Varieties of Religious Experience* gives us a clue to James's intent. The book itself is one long plea that religious experience is pervasive. Taking his examples from all areas of organized religion, James again and again ostensively makes this point—there is simply no ignoring the amount of "evidence" for religious experience. For the same reason, that is, the pervasiveness of religion, no finished formula is available. "The word 'religion' cannot stand for any single principle or essence, but is rather a collective name."[1] This plea for the richness of religious experience is negatively expressed in James's harsh critiques against vicious intellectualism in religion: "The intellectualism in religion which I wish to discredit . . . assumes to construct religious objects out of . . . logical reason alone. . . . It reaches [its conclusions] in an *a priori* way" (*VRE*, 342–43). And again, "In all sad sincerity I think we must conclude that the attempt to demonstrate by purely intellectual processes the truth of the deliverances of direct religious experience is absolutely hopeless" (ibid., 359).

There was, in James's opinion, no one formula that could contain the whole of religious experience. Any such dogmatic statement would have been diametrically opposed to his unfinished universe. On the other hand, James, at least in the final chapters of this work, does attempt some sort of justification as to why one should opt for religious experience. However, that summation, which stresses the richness and intensity of the religious experience, is tempered by the "latent" realization that all summations are suspect, to the extent that they surrender uniqueness and originality.

The pervasiveness of religious experience is evident early in *VRE*, as can be seen in the following attempt to define religion: "Religion, whatever it is, is a man's total reaction upon life, so why not say that any total reaction upon life is a religion?" (ibid., 36). And again, religion is *"the feelings, acts and experiences of individual men in their solitude, so far as they apprehend themselves to stand in relation to whatever they may consider the divine"* (ibid., 34). Here we can observe clearly the "extensity" of religious experience. One must react for the same reason that one is forced to make moral decisions—there is no possibility of being neutral.

In the beginning of the text, James argues against the attempts of "medical materialism" to explain religious experience by explaining it *away*, that is, deriving religious experience from a more ultimate neurological base. Melancholy, for example, should not be explained as due to nothing but bad digestion. Rather "by their fruits you shall know them." Or, religion is what religion does. One can detect a nascent form of pragmatism in this plea. The emphasis should be not on "root causes" but rather on the future effects of undergoing a religious experience. In opposition to reductive accounts or to those that stress one specific feature as "essential" to religion, James's outlook stresses pluralism and personal over institutional experience. Any total reaction, for James, would be "religious." And the criteria used to measure total reactions are richness and intensity. Let us first look at the richness of the religious life.

Acting as a psychologist interested in the religious experience of a person rather than in any organized religion, James continually connects this religious experience with the subliminal area of consciousness:

> we cannot, I think, avoid the conclusion that in religion we have a department of human nature with unusually close relations to the trans-marginal or subliminal region. . . . [The subliminal region] . . . is obviously the larger part of each of us, for it is the abode of everything that is latent and the reservoir of everything that passes unrecorded or unobserved. . . . [E]xperiences making their entrance through . . . [this] door have had emphatic influence in shaping religious history. (*VRE*, 381)

We are reminded here of the development of the stream of consciousness in terms of an ongoing focus/fringe continuum and also of James's metaphysical position that experience always comes to us "fringed by a more." His interest in religion is partially based on the fact that the religious person is constantly striving to acknowledge this peripheral aspect of his or her consciousness. In religion, a person becomes conscious that this

*higher part is coterminous and continuous with a more of the same quality, which is operative*
*in the universe outside him, and which he can keep in working touch with, and in a fashion get*
*on board of and save himself when all his lower being has gone to pieces in the wreck.* (*VRE*, 400)

For the religious person, the sensible world is only part of a more spiritual one, with which she is continually trying to achieve harmony. It is this quest for a more enriched experience in religion, this attempt to get at the subliminal region of consciousness, that James found so enticing. In *The Principles of Psychology (PP)*, James continually argued against the "vicious intellectualism" that dismissed certain aspects of consciousness. This attempt to take into account the subliminal regions of consciousness was paramount for James, and he found religious experience dealing with those very aspects. While it is true that origin in the subliminal region "is no infallible credential" and that whatever experience does originate there must "run the gauntlet of confrontation with the total context of experience" (*VRE*, 338), it is nonetheless the case that a religious attitude does deal with the richness of experience:

Weight, movement, velocity, direction, position, what thin, pallid, uninteresting
ideas! How could the richer animistic aspects of Nature, the peculiarities and
oddities that make phenomena picturesquely striking or expressive, fail to
have been first singled out and followed by philosophy as the more promising
avenue to the knowledge of Nature's life? Well, it is still in these richer
animistic and dramatic aspects that religion delights to dwell. (ibid., 392)

In brief, one reason that James finds religious experience so worthwhile is that it consistently remains open to the richness of experience. As a psychologist, he expressed this in terms of a religious consciousness dealing with the subliminal. Consciousness is fringed by a more; religion deals with that "more." As a result, religious experience enables one to build a richer experience:

Among the buildings out of religion which the mind spontaneously
indulges in, the aesthetic motive must never be forgotten. . . . Although
some persons aim most at intellectual purity and simplification, for others, *richness* is the supreme imaginative requirement. (*VRE*, 362)

The variety of James's demonstrations and his emphasis on vagueness leave no doubt as to which of the two options (that is, animated versus nonanimated nature) he would choose. Religious experience is enriching; it is forever in quest of the "more," the "ever not quite" of experience.

But this again is only half the story. Not only is richness to be found in religious experience, but intensity is also located there. Elsewhere, James states that the "universe is no longer, then, a mere *It* to us, but a *Thou,* if we are religious."[2] A human being, in responding to the presence of a Thou, lives life intensely. The emotion encountered in a religious experience "overcomes temperamental melancholy and imparts endurance to the Subject, or a zest, or a meaning, or an enchantment and glory to the common objects of life." (*VRE*, 397–98).

Precisely because the religious experience deals with the marginal, the fringe, the more, etc., it is demanding. The religious person, whose reaction to life is "total," is necessarily taking a chance. He is "betting on" the ideal impulses that come from his or her subliminal region. He is willing to chance giving up a present moment for a vaguely held ideal: "A man's conscious wit and will, so far as they strain toward the ideal, are aiming at something only dimly and inaccurately imagined" (*VRE,*172). Again, we notice that the concept of "vagueness"—so useful in describing the richness of religious experience in terms of the subliminal— also serves to denote the necessity of taking a chance. Religion for James includes "a new zest, which adds itself like a gift to life" (ibid., 382). Again, in describing a religious virtue like charity, we find the notion of risk at the very center of its possible realization:

> If things are ever to move upward, someone must be ready to take the
> first step, and assume the risk of it. No one who is not willing to try
> charity, to try non-resistance as the saint who is always willing, can
> tell whether these methods will or will not succeed. (ibid., 286)

The importance of risk, zest, or intensity as a common element in all truly religious experiences constitutes the second reason that James opted for rather than against it. Religious experience is risk-filled; here it is that one can reach the heights of satisfaction or fall to the depths of despair. "Here if anywhere," James says, "is the genuinely strenuous life" (*VRE,* 210). Once again, James is acting as a psychologist, and the basis of his thought is to be found in *PP.* There one discovered a view of consciousness as selective and an articulation of self-realization in terms of success over aspiration.[3] A Stoic would simply reduce all tension, all risk, by reducing his aspirations to zero. For James, resignation was impossible; to decide not to decide was a decision: "It makes a tremendous emotional and practical difference to one whether one accept the universe in the drab discolored way of stoic resignation to necessity, or with the passionate happiness of Christian saints" (*VRE,* 41).

Growth, James realized, is dependent on tension and risk; if one is to strive for the growth of experience, for a richer life, one must take chances, one must live intensely: "No fact in human nature is more characteristic than its willingness to live on a chance. The existence of the chance makes the difference, as Edmund Gurney says, between a life of which the keynote is resignation and a life of which the keynote is hope" (*VRE*, 414).[4]

In brief, at a preliminary level, *VRE* makes three very significant points on a "manifest" level:

1. In approaching religious experience psychologically, it reminds us that James's criteria here will be the same as in *PP*—richness and intensity.
2. In terms of the first of these, religious experience is valuable because it is continually open, groping for a richer, more integrated experience.
3. In terms of intensity, religious experience continually demands involvement, zest, and chance on the part of each of us.

The "manifest content" of *VRE*, then, consists of the myriad descriptions of individual experiences by individual people, such as the "once-born" versus the "twice-born" soul, that is, the individual for whom religion comes easily and the universe makes sense versus the individual for whom evil is real and must be overcome.

Throughout the text, James is very reluctant to "sum up" the religious experience, because of his emphasis on the uniquely individualistic and the pluralistic. He is tempted by "a science of religion" and yet appalled by the very notion—especially if it were allowed to replace the primary experiences of individual people. He argues ostensively, that is, by example, over and over again, as if to prevent the reader from "summing up" the variety of individual experiences too quickly. As already mentioned, at the very end of the text, he tries for some sort of summary. In religion, the individual becomes conscious that his higher part is *"coterminous and continuous with more of the same quality, which operates in the universe outside of him, and which he can keep in working touch with, and in a fashion get on board of and save himself when all his lower being has gone to pieces in the wreck"* (*VRE*, 400). Here James is caught between a rock and a hard place. On the one hand, he wants to show what religious experiences have in common. On the other hand, he does not want to explain *away* the personal characteristics of religious experience.

This becomes most apparent in *VRE* in the chapters on mysticism. James begins these chapters in medias res, so to speak. He announces four characteristics or marks that, when contained in an experience, may justify us in calling it mystical "for the purpose of these lectures." This contextualizing should give us pause. The characteristics are not a priori concepts, nor are they inductively arrived at, in any simple Baconian fashion. We would not know where to look for examples of mysticism without these indicators. James's procedure here again is more like Clifford Geertz and his toggling back and forth between "experience-near" and "experience-distant" concepts.[5] This can be said differently by noting that the term *mysticism* was "vague" for James, that is, not subject to the law of excluded middle. We should remember this and also recall that James, in *PP*, wanted to reinstate the vague to its proper place in our experience.

Continuing in this vein, to someone "outside" the mystic experience, it is true that mystics are making a descriptive claim, which appears as "authoritative" in nature. But to someone "inside" who is having or undergoing the mystic experience, her position is indubitable. As Henry Levinson has pointed out, the mystic is "confessing" not "professing," that is, not making a normal truth-claim.[6] She is being tenacious in holding on to her belief, which cannot be cast into doubt. She may be irrational, given our definition of rationality. However, she does not think she is irrational; it may well be the case that she is not self-conscious at all. She may be aware, but her awareness may not be subject to propositional logic. More on this below.

The mystic confessing is a *first-person* account. The mystic who is put in jail and asked to describe her experiences later is rendering a *third-person account*. It is an attempt to change someone's mind who has not had several mystical experiences. As mentioned, James oscillates back and forth between the first-person and the third-person account, rather like the anthropologist Geertz, who is constantly trying to see things from the point of view of the "other"—all the time realizing that the anthropologist cannot completely "go native." James has, by his own admission, not had a mystic experience, but he is trying to see things from the mystic's point of view. In other words, James is trying to read the mystics "sympathetically." This could be viewed as a psychological rather than a logical point, but it could also be seen as redefining the term logical so as to include use of empathy. James's capacity to enter into a sympathetic understanding of the experience of others was remarkable. The account presented here is a "sympathetic" interpretation of James's own text, one extending to James what he extended to others. It may also contain a redefinition of the term *knowledge*. Going further, first-person accounts and third-person accounts are not so much *incompatible* as they are *incommensurate* with one another. It is not that the first-person account is right and the third-person account is wrong or that they contradict each other, but, rather, that they have different ideas about what it is to be right and, equally important, have no agreement in advance about how to reach such an agreement.

In *VRE*, James states that mystical experiences "open out the possibilities of other orders of truth" (*VRE*, 335). On the one hand, we should remember that he wanted to develop a "science of religions." On the other hand, James has told us that "the attempt to demonstrate by purely intellectual processes the truth of the deliverances of direct religious experience is absolutely hopeless" (ibid., 359).

This much being said, James sometimes does seem to lean too much in one direction over the other. That is, he sometimes seems tempted to clean up the vague and to get rid of the latent. For example, he suggests that the "overcoming of all the universal barriers between the individual and the Absolute is the great mystic achievement. In mystic states we both become one with the Absolute and we become aware of our oneness. This is the everlasting and triumphant mystical tradition, hardly altered by differences of clime or creed" (*VRE,* 332). Or, as a second example, take James's statement that the "incommunicableness of the transport is the keynote of all mysticism" (ibid., 331). It seems at times that James was tempted by "experience-distant" concepts to "universalize" a definition of mysticism, to essentialize it too much. On the other hand, James retracts the first of these statements a mere four pages later, noting that he has tidied up too much, that is, arrived at too permanent a conclusion:

> But even this presumption from the unanimity of mystics is far from being strong. In characterizing mystic states as pantheistic, optimistic, etc, I am afraid I over-simplified the truth. I did so for expository reasons, and to keep the closer to the classic mystical tradition. The classic religious mysticism, it now must be confessed, is only a "privileged case." It is an *extract,* kept true to type by the selection of the fittest specimens. (ibid., 336)

It seems that what has occurred here is that various examples of the mystic experience, initially used as "crude analogies," have turned sour. This refers to Margaret Masterman's brilliant article on Thomas Kuhn, titled "The Nature of a Paradigm," and her description of a paradigm as a "crude analogy"—as it is *used:* "A crude analogy is finite in extensibility. . . . it is incompatible with any other crude analogy. . . . it is extensible only by an inferential process of 'replication' . . . but not by the normal methods of examining inference."[7] The analogy, qua analogy, turns sour when it is overextended or pushed too far. How far is too far can only come with practice, that is, when the paradigm generates a "significant" anomaly.

It is worth remembering that James admits that we do not know what we are doing, that we must collect mystical "facts" sympathetically, hoping that some form of understanding of mystical states will occur in the future. In "A Suggestion about Mysticism," his last article, James says, "we know so little of the noetic value of abnormal mental states of any kind that in my own opinion we had better keep an open mind and collect facts sympathetically for a long time to come.

We shall not *understand* these alterations of consciousness either in this generation or in the next."[8] We are, then, groping; perhaps this is "faith seeking understanding." We hope to understand, even though our hope may not be justified.

The first two characteristics of mystic experiences are their ineffable and noetic qualities. The other two, transiency and passivity, while "typical," seem to
be neither necessary nor sufficient. But the two characteristics of ineffability and
noesis are suspicious of each other. *Ineffable* suggests something beyond discourse
or articulation; *noetic* says that something is learned or disclosed in a mystical experience. In addition, there is no "essence" of ineffability. Ineffability is not a single
universal experience; it is uniquely flavored by the specific context.

Given James's emphasis on the personal and on feeling in *VRE*, it may well be
the case that language has multiple functions in that text. The primary use of language may not be descriptive or propositional. For James, in *VRE*, is trying to say
the unsayable, that is, the ineffable. He is using language to disclose, not describe,
the inability of language to catch the ineffable. He is much more conscious of this
in *A Pluralistic Universe (PU)* where he says,

> As long as one continues *talking*, intellectualism remains in undisturbed
> possession of the field. The return to life can't come about by talking. It is
> an *act*; to make you return to life, I must set an example for your imita-
> tion, I must deafen you to talk. . . . Or I must *point*, point to the mere *that* of
> life, and you by inner sympathy must fill out the *what* for yourselves.[9]

In *VRE*, James says that "in mystical literature, such self-contradictory phrases
as 'dazzling obscurity,' [and] 'whispering silence' . . . are continually met with.
They prove that not conceptual speech, but music rather, is the element through
which we are best spoken to by mystical truth. Many mystical scriptures are indeed little more than musical compositions" (333). Ellen Suckiel suggests that
"[i]n making this claim, James is not suggesting that mystical experience is non-
cognitive. Rather, he is invoking a notion of understanding which is more primary
than propositional understanding."[10] Furthermore, one may not always be able to
articulate completely what is known at this level. It is, after all, *ineffable*. Suckiel
asks, "Why *must* propositional knowledge be the only type of knowledge?"[11] In
opposition, she suggests that "the gymnast, dancer, or diver develops a kinesthetic
self-awareness, and through experience and attention to that experience, has a
sense, not reducible to a set of propositions, of the appropriate timing and effort
required for various maneuvers."[12]

Finally, the element of "transiency," the third mark of mystical experience,
is perhaps a bit more important than James realized—even though he does call it

"typical." If transiency received more emphasis, the pluralism or vagueness inherent in mysticism might become more apparent. An experience *remembered* is not the same as an experience *had* or *undergone*, even if it is remembered as authoritative. Also, a "remembered" experience is a self-conscious experience, as opposed to one wherein one is merely, or completely, "conscious." The remembered experience both is and is not continuous with the actual experience, and the line between the two is vague—just as, for James, the line between percepts and concepts, or knowledge by acquaintance versus knowledge about, is vague.

In sum, the manifest content of *VRE* consists in the rich descriptive accounts of a vast panorama of individual experiences. These are sometimes described as having to do with being coterminous with a "more" that we can get in touch with. But the emphasis on the personal and the unique keeps James a bit uneasy about generalizations. This is most evident in the sections on mysticism, an important topic because it functions as an "exemplar" of what James will later call "pure experience." The latent content of *VRE* becomes more manifest as he and the reader realize the futility of providing any *complete* science of religions. One must, given the limitations of language, be satisfied with "crude analogies."

# 5

## Pragmatism

### Corridor as "Latent" and "The Will to Believe"

Like many of his other texts, James's *Pragmatism (Prag)* contains both a manifest and a latent image. On the surface level, it is a "method only." James describes it as a corridor with various topics leading to different rooms by our asking "What difference does it make?" if a given theory is true. It is a way of resolving issues rather than dissolving them. James's pragmatism differed from that of his colleague Charles Sanders Peirce who saw pragmatism as a way of dissolving issues, that is, explaining them *away*. In suggesting that "an idea is true if it makes a difference," James offered a theory of truth fundamentally different from the paradigm offered by René Descartes, for whom knowledge was equated with certainty. Let us see how James develops his position.

To begin with, we should note what pragmatism was supposed to do. In an era that had become one of scientific positivism, the place of the romantic in a theory of truth was indeed a perilous one. The division existed in philosophy between those who were tenderhearted and those who were hard-nosed, with the understanding that these were mutually exclusive. With the rise of positivism, James laments,

> The romantic spontaneity and courage are gone, the vision is material-
> istic and depressing. Ideals appear as inert by-products of physiology; what
> is higher is explained by what is lower and treated forever as a case of
> "nothing but"—nothing but something else of a quite inferior sort.[1]

The reaction to this, on the other hand, "dwelt on so high a level of abstraction that . . . it is compatible with any state of things whatever being true here below" (*Prag*, 19). James's answer to this dilemma was to "offer the oddly named thing pragmatism as a philosophy that can satisfy both kinds of demands" (ibid., 23). Important here are precisely the two things James is trying to put together (or better, refusing to allow being torn apart). Reductive materialism is almost synonymous with the impoverishment of experience, but it had the positive quality of being useful or "pragmatic." Romantic idealism, however, had no cutting edge. It led nowhere—in short, it had no intensity. On the other hand, it was richer than a simple reductionism, although its richness can lead to dualism and to absolutes. Pragmatism, as offered by James, is an attempt to do justice both to richness and to intensity as they are found in everyday experience.

What, then, is the pragmatic method, and how does it work? In *Prag*, James asserts that

> To attain perfect clearness in our thought of an object, . . . we need only consider what conceivable effects of a practical kind the object may involve—what sensations we are to expect from it, and what reactions we must prepare. Our conception of these effects, whether immediate or remote, is then for us the whole of our conception of the object, so far as the conception has positive significance at all. (29)

Ideas are true if they have a "worthwhile leading." They must be seen as hypotheses, as projections. As such, they point beyond themselves to verifications in experience. Because of this, ideas are not self-contained; they are interpenetrative with sensations:

> *True ideas are those that we can assimilate, validate, corroborate and verify. False ideas are those that we cannot.* . . . Truth *happens* to an idea. It *becomes* true, is *made* true by events. Its verity *is* in fact an event, a process: the process namely of its verifying itself, its veri-*fication*. Its validity is the process of its vali-*dation*. (*Prag*, 97)

This process of verifying consists in bringing out the concrete worth of an idea:

> You must bring out of each word its practical cash-value, set it at work within the stream of your experience. It appears less as a solution then, than as a program for more work, and more particularly as an indication of the ways in which existing realities may be *changed*.
> *Theories thus become instruments, not answers to enigmas, in which we can rest.* (*Prag*, 31–32)

Any given idea, then, is actually a process—it takes time. To formulate an idea is not to come up with a finished product but merely with a plan of action. An idea must agree, or it must lead to somewhere useful:

To "agree" in the widest sense with a reality *can only mean to be guided either straight up to it or into its surroundings, or to be put into such working touch with it as to handle either it or something connected with it better than if we disagreed.* (*Prag,* 102)

These quotes emphasize the intensity of experience. Ideas must have a cutting edge; they must make a difference. They imply that there is no such thing as an impartial idea. There are only ideas for me, for you, etc. These statements about making a difference seemingly advocate a subjective approach. Since James refused to set up any one discipline (science, religion, psychology, etc.) as the judge "of making a difference," the pragmatic theory of truth seems at first glance to be a simple plea for subjectivism—supposedly saying "this idea is true because it makes a difference to me right now."

On further reflection, however, we see that this opinion is quite incorrect; rather, here, as in other places, the subject-object dichotomy is simply insufficient to do justice to the Jamesian outlook. The following text illustrates this well:

Primarily . . . the truth of a state of mind means . . . [the] function of *a leading that is worthwhile.* When a moment in our experience, of any kind whatever, inspires us with a thought that is true, that means that sooner or later we dip by that thought's guidance into the particulars of experience again and make advantageous connection with them. . . . Our experience meanwhile is all shot through with regularities. One bit of it can warn us to get ready for another bit, and "intend" or be "significant of" that remoter object. The object's advent is the significance's verification. Truth, in these cases, meaning nothing but eventual verification, is manifestly incompatible with waywardness on our part. (*Prag,* 98–99)

Two points seem evident here. First, ideas must make a difference, and making a difference must be viewed as involving human needs, desires, wants, etc. In other words, an experience that makes a difference is an "intense" experience. But, second, experience is extensive as well as intensive. It is cumulative as well as consummatory.

The following quotes in *Prag* should be seen and taken together:

In our cognitive as well as in our active life we are creative. We *add,* both to the subject and to the predicate, part of reality. The world stands really malleable, waiting to receive its final touches at our hands. Like the kingdom of heaven, it suffers human violence willingly. Man *engenders* truths upon it. (123)

Woe to him whose beliefs play fast and loose with the order which realities follows in his experience; they will lead him nowhere or else make false connections. (99)

Life is intense, zestful, etc., because a person structures and molds it. Experience is plastic. In a real sense, we have no choice—we are condemned to create:

What shall we call a *thing* anyhow? It seems quite arbitrary, for we carve out everything, just as we carve out constellations to suit our human purposes. . . . We break the flux of sensible reality into things . . . at our will. We create the subjects of our true as well as of our false propositions. . . . [Y]ou can't weed out the human contribution. (*Prag*, 122)

This emphasis on personal effort is undoubtedly a vitally important one in James's philosophical outlook. Again and again, he reminds us of the fact that man or woman is basically an artist:

What we say about reality . . . depends on the perspective into which we throw it. The *that* of it is its own; but the *what* depends on the *which;* and the which depends on *us*. . . . *Even* in the field of sensation, our minds exert a certain arbitrary choice. By our inclusions and omissions we trace the field's extent; by our emphasis we mark its foreground and its background; by our order we read it in this direction or in that. We receive in short the block of marble, but we carve the statue ourselves. This applies to the "eternal" parts of reality as well: we shuffle our perceptions of intrinsic relation and arrange them just as freely. We read them in one serial order or another, class them in this way or that, treat one or the other as more fundamental, until our beliefs about them form those bodies of truth known as logics, geometries, or arithmetics, in each and all of which the form and order in which the whole is cast is flagrantly man-made. (*Prag*, 118–19)

On the other hand, a person is responsible for learning from her past experiences. One aspect without the other is inadequate. Indeed, the very use of language to articulate the situation runs the risk of misleading us. So, here, simply to say an idea must have a "leading quality" about it is inadequate because, conceptually, we divorce the idea from its terminus and "one-idea-and-leading" from "another-idea-and-its-leading." In the concrete world, however, these leadings are consummatory.

In brief, the intensity of ideas in the pragmatic method is well illustrated by the Jamesian vision of man or woman as an artist. But the organic richness of the pragmatic method is seen if we realize that it is an ongoing and cumulative method, that a person tries to be *continually* creative in and through the matrix of experience. James is equally concerned with this cumulative aspect of "making a difference": "New truth is always a go-between, a smoother-over of transitions. It marries old opinion to new fact, so as ever to show a minimum of jolt, a maximum of continuity" (*Prag*, 35).

Older truths, then, are important: "Loyalty to them is the first principle" (*Prag*, 35). But past ideas are only part of "reality." They must be taken together with the novel situation being presently encountered. It is because we can contain so much of our past in cold storage via concepts that we have the ability to respond to the present situation, to harness experience to our needs and wants:

> Our minds thus grow in spots; and like grease spots, the spots spread. But we let them spread as little as possible: we keep unaltered as much of our old knowledge, as many of our old prejudices and beliefs, as we can. We patch and tinker more than we renew. The novelty soaks in; it stains the ancient mass; but it is also tinged by what absorbs it. Our past apperceives and co-operates; and in the new equilibrium in which each step forward in the process of learning terminates, it happens relatively seldom that the new fact is added *raw*. More usually it is embedded cooked, as one might say, or stewed down in the sauce of the old.
>
> New truths thus are resultants of new experiences and of old truths combined and mutually modifying one another. (*Prag*, 83)

This picture of knowledge, then, as articulated in *Prag*, is an ever-shifting yet cumulative appropriation. Truth, defined as agreeable leading, "grafts itself on previous truth, modifying it in the process" (116). And "[t]he marriage of fact and theory is endlessly fertile" (101). Ideas must make a difference; therefore, the real datum is this idea-and-this-projected difference, that idea-with-that-projected difference, etc. As these slide into the past, they serve to modify new data, either negatively or positively. Always, however, the notion of making a difference is seen as involving both extensity and intensity. The object is to keep as much of the past as possible and still deal with the intensity of the present novel situation:

> Man's beliefs at any time are so much experience *funded*. . . . Truths emerge from facts; but they dip forward into facts again and add to them; which facts again create or reveal new truth (the word is indifferent) and so on indefinitely. . . . The case is like a snow-ball's growth, due as it is to the distribution of the snow on the one hand, and to the successive pushes of the boys on the other, with these factors co-determining each other incessantly. (*Prag*, 107–108)

A person does not simply have perceptual copies of the world—she or he engenders truth on it. On the other hand, a person's creation is temporal, cumulative, not an instantaneous out-flowing. A little reflection will show that even the word *fact* here is an idealization, since, once the process is started, we "hardly take in an impression at all, in the absence of a preconception of what impressions there may possibly be" (ibid., 119).

Precisely because richness and intensity are taken together, no absolute theory is allowed: "no theory is absolutely a transcript of reality, but . . . any one of them may from some point of view be useful. Their great use is to summarize old facts and lead to new ones" (*Prag,* 33). Pragmatism leans toward pluralism but a concatenated pluralism: "'The world is one' . . . just so far as we experience it to be concatenated, one by as many definite conjunctions as appear. But then also *not* one by just as many definite *dis*-junctions as we find" (ibid., 73).

We may select any one of a series of ways in which the world could be called one—one in terms of one cause, one in terms of one knower, one in terms of one purpose, etc. Each of these is precisely that—a selection, based on interests, needs, and a desire, in short, to live life more intensely. Because each conceptualization is made for a particular need, all these conceptualizations remain possibilities: "Possibilities obtain in our [pragmatic] world; in the absolute world, where all that is *not* is from eternity impossible, and all that *is* is necessary, the category of possibility has no application" (*Prag,* 127).

This, then, is the manifest content of *Prag.* It is described metaphorically as a wedding, that is, "marriage" of new fact to old opinion so as to maximize continuity and minimize jolt. James also describes it as a "corridor": "at the outset at least . . . [pragmatism] stands for no particular results. It has no dogmas and no doctrines save its method. . . . it lies in the midst of our theories like a corridor in a hotel. Innumerable chambers open out of it" (ibid., 32).

However, the use of this metaphor by James serves as an entryway into the latent content of *Prag,* as does the subtle entrance of "The Will to Believe" into *Prag* in lecture six, "Pragmatism's Conception of Truth." Let us see how this comes about.

The corridor metaphor is arguably the most famous one associated with pragmatism. Unfortunately, it is often not taken (and perhaps was not even offered) as a metaphor at all. Taken in a positivistic sense as a description rather than a metaphor, the corridor can be appropriated as the metaphor to end all metaphors, the story to end all stories, the ultimate metanarrative. It promotes the view of pragmatism as neutral, as not value-laden, as not in itself a theory among theories.

And this in spite of James's own admonition, just a few pages earlier in the text, that philosophy "is only partly got from books; it is our individual way of just seeing and feeling the total push and pressure of the cosmos" (*Prag*, 9). And again: "The history of philosophy is to a great extent that of a certain clash of human temperaments" (ibid., 11). John Smith long ago pointed to this reference in James as one that can cause extreme difficulty:

> The corridor represents the method and what goes on in the individual rooms represents "doctrines" as distinct from the method. The pragmatists were somewhere uncritical in their acceptance of this distinction; they seemed to think that to specify a method does not involve presuppositions concerning what there is and what there must be if the method is to prove successful. . . . The underlying problem is of the utmost importance because of the widespread belief to be found not only among philosophers but among scientists as well that there is a "neutral" way of proceeding which is unencumbered by the biases inevitably expressed in "doctrines."[2]

Ironically, the corridor metaphor appropriated in this way so as to invoke final closure allows James's *Prag* to function like Descartes's *Meditations*. The latter was offered to the reader by its author as the "story to end all stories." As Alasdair MacIntyre has noted,

> Descartes . . . having abjured history as a means to truth, recounts to us his own history as the medium through which the search for truth is to be carried on. . . . Yet Descartes radically misdescribes his own crises and thus has proved a highly misleading guide to the nature of epistemological crises in general. . . . Descartes' doubt is contextless doubt. . . . He does not recognize that among the features of the universe which he is not putting into doubt is his own capacity not only to use the French and the Latin languages, but even to express the same thought in both languages.[3]

Descartes's failure to note the biases of language in general has a more particular parallel in not noting the biases of linguistic metaphor. The metaphor of the corridor, when taken literally, functions in a contextless fashion—as opposed to an interpretive one that both reveals and conceals. Descartes's approach enabled him, supposedly, to call everything into question all at once. Taking the corridor metaphor as literally accurate has the same effect, that is, it assumes that there is a position where nothing is taken for granted. However, this metaphor should not be allowed to function in a seemingly neutral fashion; nor, on the other hand, should it be inordinately privileged over others.

Several James scholars have highlighted James's constant use of metaphor. Stan Scott, for example, states that "James participated in a process of shifting paradigms for the study of the mind, and in that process he found metaphor to be an indispensable part of his thinking method. . . . He appears to have accepted the premise that to understand is to generate metaphors of understanding."[4] Metaphors, for Scott, do not disclose their meaning in a straightforward manner. Rather, they are "a way of understanding a phenomenon by means of indirection."[5] For Charlene Haddock Seigfried also, James's style is no mere accident: "William James's use of analogy and metaphor is more than a rhetorical device. It is integral to his hermeneutics and reflects his concrete analysis of human thinking."[6] Like Nietzsche's use of aphorisms, the meaning and conditions of James's metaphors are not immediately apparent, but rather require an art of exegesis: "Metaphors better reflect . . . contextuality and revisability of discourse than discursive language does."[7] In short, metaphors should be taken as *interpretations*, rather than descriptions. This is part of the latent content of *Prag.*

As stated previously, "The Will to Believe" sneaks into *Prag* in lecture six, "Pragmatism's Conception of Truth." On the surface, the subject of the lecture is to explain what it means to say that an idea is true if it "agrees" with reality. James is at pains to indicate that agreement does not exclusively or necessarily mean "copying" (*Prag*, 96). An idea is true if it copes with the present moment, while preserving as much of the past as possible. Facts must be taken account of, as well as abstract "kinds" (for example, geometry), together with the entire body of previous truths already in our possession (ibid., 102–103). Going further, an idea must be not only meaningful (comprehensible) and verifiable; it must be the *type* of verifiability required by the present situation. James says, "If you ask me what o'clock it is and I tell you that I live at 95 Irving Street, my answer may indeed be true, but you don't see why it is my duty to give it. A false address would be as much to the purpose" (ibid., 111). In short, James, having given up the old "objective" standard of truth as correspondence, is busy defining what a true idea— that is, one that works—looks like: "It must derange common sense and previous belief as little as possible, and it must lead to some sensible terminus or other that can be verified exactly. To 'work' means both these things" (ibid., 104). This is an iteration of the marriage metaphor, *stressing* continuity. It would result in a "concatenated" (ibid., 73), that is, strung-along universe, one still pluralistic in nature. For the most part, it is the job of the philosopher to preserve and nurture as "thick" a picture as is possible, rather than allowing any single abstract account to achieve final closure.

But, even when these instructions are carried out, the situation sometimes remains indeterminate. Sometimes even when the sensory and the conceptual and the historical are allowed for, there remains something to be decided—

and this can only be done on "preferential" grounds. James says, "Yet sometimes alternative theoretic formulas are equally compatible with all the truths we know, and then we choose between them for subjective reasons. We choose the kind of theory to which we are already partial; we follow 'elegance' or 'economy'" (*Prag*, 104). In this picture presented by James, then, sometimes we assume responsibility for selecting one domain *over* another. In short, we choose for "sentimental" reasons, or we exercise "the will to believe."

In sum, *Prag* has both a latent and a manifest content. On the surface, it appears as mere description. But its latent content surfaces in several different ways. First, as we have seen, a corridor image can be taken either literally or metaphorically. Taken literally, it aspires to be a neutral description or portrayal of experience. Taken metaphorically, the corridor both reveals and conceals simultaneously, thereby compelling the reader to interpret, to engage with the text, and to commit herself. Second, "The Will to Believe" creeps into *Prag* at a certain juncture, revealing that sometimes more than perception and conception are involved in calling an idea "true." While this does not occur all the time, it does occur at important moments. There is a third sense in which the text of *Prag* hides a latent content. This becomes apparent when we contrast the opening and closing lectures with the six lectures between them. Here James deals with tragedy and death. This is taken up below in the conclusion.

For now, let us note that pragmatism is not metaphysically neutral. It has metaphysical presuppositions or commitments about the universe itself—viewing it as unfinished, pluralistic, and concatenated, and both inviting and requiring participation by each of us. Let us, therefore, turn to the development of James's metaphysics as this takes place in *Essays in Radical Empiricism* and *A Pluralistic Universe*.

# 6
## Metaphysics
### *Radical Empiricism and Pure Experience*

## *Essays in Radical Empiricism*

As is well known, in *The Principles of Psychology (PP)* James adopted a functional dualism, between psychology and philosophy, or thought and reality. However, his description of consciousness as selective and intentional was a "nascent attack" on the subject-object dichotomy. For several years after, James struggled with the issue of how to reject this dualistic division. His answer, tentative as it is, is contained in *Essays in Radical Empiricism (ERE)*. For it is here that James introduces the notion of "pure experience."

Let us commence by recalling exactly what "radical empiricism" is, as James himself verbalized it in the preface to *The Meaning of Truth (MT)*:

> Radical empiricism consists first of a postulate, next of a statement of fact, and finally of a generalized conclusion.
>
> The postulate is that the only things that shall be debatable among philosophers shall be things definable in terms drawn from experience. . . .
>
> The statement of fact is that the relations between things, conjunctive as well as disjunctive, are just as much matters of direct particular experience, neither more so nor less so, than the things themselves.
>
> The generalized conclusion is that therefore the parts of experience hold together from next to next by relations that are themselves parts of experience. The directly apprehended universe needs, in short, no extraneous trans-empirical connective support, but possesses in its own right a concatenated or continuous structure.[1]

In the *ERE* James asserts that reality is *richer* than we have realized; it contains not only substantive parts but also transitive ones, and the latter may be of either a disjunctive or a conjunctive nature. In short, at first glance it seems that James extends his analysis of the stream of consciousness (as found in *PP*) to the stage where it describes *reality* in general. Indeed, there is much truth in this; a great deal that James has to say about consciousness as a continuously changing stream with all sorts of relational fringes, he also has to say about reality in *ERE*. An overly hasty conclusion might well be that reality *is* consciousness or, less hasty but still wrong, that consciousness is the *foundation* or basis for this description of reality.

But James, having asserted that, for anything to be considered in philosophy, it must be capable of being experienced, now asks, "How is consciousness experienced?" And he gives a pragmatic answer. To the question "What difference does it make if I say 'A is conscious of B' as opposed to 'A is next to B'?" James replies that A is conscious of B if and only if there is a series of intimate, conjunctive transitions between the intermediaries of A and B, through which A goes, saying "ah ha," "yes," "yes," "ah ha," etc., until he or she reaches the stage of having a vague intention fulfilled, of actually "seeing" that which s/he had in mind.[2] Consciousness, in short, is a function for James; it is not a substance. It is the function of an intimate, agreeable leading. Most important, it is not found as separate at the primary level of experience, but rather arises retrospectively as an addition. The present moment is not simply conscious; it becomes conscious insofar as it is affiliated with other moments in the past:

> We must remember that no dualism of being represented and representing
> resides in the experience per se. In its pure state, or when isolated, there
> is no self-splitting of it into conscious and what the consciousness is "of."
> Its subjectivity and objectivity are functional attributes solely, realized only
> when the experience is "taken," i.e., talked of, twice, considered along with
> its two differing contexts respectively, by a new retrospective experience,
> of which that whole past complication now forms the fresh content.
>     The instant field of the present is at all times what I call the "pure" experi-
> ence. It is only virtually or potentially either object or subject as yet. (*ERE*, 13)

This text carries several important points. First of all, the subject-object distinction, or the consciousness-content distinction, does not arise at the primordial level of experience but can only be ascertained by turning from or "bracketing" reality, defined here as the present. When reality is so bracketed, then the relation between consciousness and its object can be described, as has been done above, in terms of intimate conjunctive transitions. Furthermore, there is a "relativism" in-volved here; what functions as consciousness in one context might well function as the object of consciousness in another. A given moment of experience can be counted twice over after it drops into the past; it can function as both conscious-ness and as content of consciousness. It follows from this position that we are never immediately conscious *that* we are conscious or, in other words, that we are never immediately self-conscious. Consciousness of self, like consciousness of any other object-for-consciousness, is only retrospectively available.

In *Pragmatism (Prag)*, James quoted sympathetically Søren Kierkegaard's state-ment that "we live forwards . . . but we understand backwards."[3] The situation is no different, and is indeed crucially important, at the metaphysical level. And it is precisely here that James's views on language provide a key insight. As he noted in the above quote from *ERE*, the subject-object distinction only arises when ex-perience is talked about. Though language is necessary, there is a sense in which language betrays. This is particularly true when one is trying to allude to the ques-tion of reality or, in James's terms, to pure experience. With some suspicions of language in mind, then, let us turn to James's portrayals of pure experience. In "Does 'Consciousness' Exist?" James says,

> My thesis is that if we start with the supposition that there is only one primal stuff or material in the world, a stuff of which everything is composed, and if we call that stuff "pure experience," then knowing can easily be explained as a particular sort of rela-tion towards one another into which portions of pure experience may enter. (*ERE*, 4)

Elsewhere in *ERE*, he tells us that the "principle of pure experience is . . . a meth-odological postulate" (ibid., 81).

The statement that there was one "stuff" of experience was to cause James trouble, but even by the end of the article, he had anticipated this, telling the reader that he had so spoken only for the sake of fluency and that "there is no *gen-eral* stuff of which experience at large is made. There are as many stuffs as there are 'natures' in the things experienced" (*ERE*, 14). James's intent seems clear, though his verbalizations of it are causing him difficulty. Pure experience here is neither a "many" nor a "one" but is rather the state of the universe before these two emerge as alternatives. In *Prag*, James has the same problem: he cannot ac-cept monism, so terms his own outlook "pluralistic"—almost by default. But ac-tually, as he sometimes realized, his own outlook is, again, neither a monism nor a pluralism, but rather a view of reality as "concatenated."[4] Similar difficulties arise with the attempt to verbalize pure experience as beneath the consciousness-content distinction, the percept-concept distinction,[5] and the past-present-future distinction, as we shall see below. In short, James, having asserted the existence of something beneath these various dichotomies, is having great difficulty "catching" it in language. On the other hand, he must say something; he must be careful not to let pure experience lapse into a supernatural entity or a transcendental category. A strong tenet of radical empiricism is that all things termed "existing" be experienceable. We return to this issue of describing pure experience below.

In the above quotes, James views pure experience as a "thesis" and a "methodological postulate." Clearly, then, his metaphysical outlook is not foundationalist in tone and this (nonfoundational) aspect is essential. There is no apodictic ground to the Jamesian outlook. *Even his own position* is to be taken as a hypothesis. It must be affirmed, not presented as a "solved solution" to the issue of being or reality.

"Pure experience" is a postulate, but it is so in a very *realistic* sense; it points beyond itself. Metaphysically speaking, reality is broader than the known; pure experience represents an attempt by James to get at, or disclose, reality. The latter is not an object, since pure experience describes an ontological situation that is prior to the subject-object dichotomy. "Pure experience" is a concept that refers to pure experience in the same way that, for Paul Tillich, "God" is a symbol for God. A symbol, for Tillich, "points beyond itself while participating in that to which it points."[6] Gerald Myers is correct, then, to have "emphasized the pictorial, visionary character of James's concept of pure experience."[7] Actually, James uses the term "pure experience" in different, overlapping ways. Let us flesh out some of its meanings.

"The instant field of the present is at all times what I call the 'pure' experience" (*ERE*, 13). James often uses this description when he is emphasizing the indeterminate given, existing prior to various dualisms that arise, such as the subject-object and consciousness-content distinctions. Similar statements are "Experience in its immediacy seems perfectly fluent" (ibid., 45); and "'Pure experience' is the name which I gave to the immediate flux of life which furnishes the material to our later reflection with its conceptual categories" (ibid., 46). Here James tries to portray what is *immediately* given, but the irony is that what is immediately given is *not* immediate—it is flux, and qua flux it is the "ground" of all future statements. The present moment is *really* the passing moment.[8] As Eugene Fontinell has said,

> While everyone might agree that what is immediately experienced is beyond dispute, it is quite evident that just what it is that is immediately experienced is a matter of great dispute. This is made obvious by the variety of competing, inconsis-

tent, and even contradictory claims of immediate experience. James and a host of twentieth-century phenomenologists have significantly deepened our awareness of how difficult it is to describe with complete fidelity the characteristics of experience. There would be no such difficulty if immediate experience were clear, distinct, and unambiguous instead of being characterized by obscurities, shades, margins, fringes, penumbras, and what James has called "the vague and inarticulate."[9]

In *ERE*, when James replies to the question "For whom is pure experience 'available'?" his answer is rather exclusionary: "Only new born babes, or men in semi-coma from sleep, drugs, illnesses, or blows, may be assumed to have an experience pure in the literal sense of a *that* which is not yet any definite *what*, tho' ready to be all sorts of 'whats'" (46). Here we have a second sense of pure experience, as describing the world as it *was*, before consciousness arose. However, it is important to realize that "pure experience," as a descriptive term for either the present moment or the past, is *itself* a conception, a secondhand experience for James. "Pure experience" cannot be taken to refer exclusively to the past, because, in such a formulation, novelty would not be real; change would not take place. James would find this position untenable. But what he also realized, though he often did not state it as clearly as he might, is that "pure experience" cannot be exclusively identified with the present—if the present is taken as immediately given—for exactly the same reasons. He verbalizes this by saying that the present *is not present*—that is, is a passing moment—or by saying that the present is an activity. In short, the key to James's different descriptions of "pure experience" here is to remember that experience "grows": "experience itself, taken at large, can grow by its edges. That one moment of it proliferates into the next by transitions which, whether conjunctive or disjunctive, continue the experimental tissue, can not, I contend, be denied" (ibid., 42).

In this more processive sense of pure experience, consciousness has arisen as a relational transition between various moments, as these have dropped into the past, achieving "objective immortality" through "prehension," to borrow A. N. Whitehead's terminology.[10] In a third sense then, "pure experience" refers neither exclusively to the present nor to the past, but rather denies that dichotomy as exclusive. "Pure experience" refers to a continually changing process in which the past enters into the present, and part of the latter's significance is as a positive or negative continuation of the past. In this formulation of "pure experience," consciousness arises by way of addition qua relation. But, once arisen, it exhibits a curious stubbornness: it cannot simply be reduced to experience again. To do so would be to deny the reality of change: "*The separation of it [pure experience] into con-*

*sciousness and content comes, not by way of subtraction, but by way of addition*—the addition, to a given concrete piece of it, of other sets of experiences, in connection with which severally its use or function may be of two different kinds" (*ERE*, 6–7).

In this third sense, consciousness has come upon the scene, with the result that "it happens relatively seldom that . . . a new fact is added *raw*. More usually it is embedded cooked, as one might say, or stewed down in the sauce of the old" (*Prag*, 83). Pure experience is a continually changing process in which the very relation of consciousness itself *adds* to the reality. This formulation transcends the present-past distinction.

But even this last linguistic formulation of "pure experience" is a conceptualization, though it refers to a level of reality beneath the exclusivity of concepts. Furthermore, James realized that, not only is this "final" conceptualization inadequate, but conceptualization *as such* is inadequate. Nonetheless conceptualization is necessary. This view is found primarily in *A Pluralistic Universe (PU)*.

### A Pluralistic Universe

Some of James's most mature statements on metaphysics are to be found in *PU*. What is often ignored, however, is the crucial role that faith and "the will to believe" play in his final position. In this section, we shall look at three topics: the setting of *PU*, the relationship of logic to reality, and the actual role philosophic systems themselves play in terms of the "faith ladder." The residual effect of these three issues is to affirm a universe where real possibility exists. James saw this and acted accordingly. Let us see how this comes about.

### The Setting of *A Pluralistic Universe*

James had originally titled this volume "The Present Situation in Philosophy," and, in the initial chapters, he sketches out three different religious choices. Theism offers a God "out there" and a basically dualistic account of the universe. Divine human activity is not an illusion; but theism, advocating as it does a God complete from all eternity, "makes us outsiders and keeps us foreigners in relation to God" (*PU*, 17). Since God and truth exist from all time, God does not come to know himself through us; we are merely passive observers. In short, theism does not allow for *possibility*. James explains this by saying that there is no intimacy between creature and creator. The formal structure of theism is such that the possibility of responding to divine invitation does not even logically exist. In theism, "God is not heart of our heart and reason of our reason, but our magistrate, rather;

and mechanically to obey his commands, however strange they may be, remains our only moral duty" (ibid.). Theism allows diversity but at too high a price: loss of any intimacy, loss of interaction, and loss of actual possibility.

Pantheism, by contrast, offers us a more intimate relationship with God. The question is at what price. James distinguishes a more intimate and a less intimate form of pantheism (*PU,* 19). The monistic form of pantheism, which James calls the "philosophy of the absolute," ultimately advocates a doctrine of internal relations. These relations between creature and creator are so intimate as to abolish all diversity whatsoever as an illusion. In contrast to this "all form," James delineates an "each form," that is, a pluralistic pantheism, which "is willing to believe that there may ultimately never be an all-form at all, that the substance of reality may never get totally collected, that some of it may remain outside of the largest combination of it ever made" (ibid., 20). Most importantly, James specifically identifies pluralistic pantheism and radical empiricism: "If we give to the monistic subspecies the name of philosophy of the absolute, we may give that of radical empiricism to its pluralistic rival" (ibid.). This identification is of no small importance, for it shows that radical empiricism is *not* neutral on the religious question.

## Logic and Reality

Reflecting on his earlier philosophic position, James recalls that, in *PP,* he could not accept a reductionist point of view of reality. For example, $H_2$-plus-O together produce a new entity, because they *"affect surrounding bodies differently"* (*PU,* 86). Note the use of the pragmatic criterion here: ideas are different if they have different effects. Similarly, James argued that consciousness of the alphabet was *not* reducible to twenty-six separate awarenesses of its specific parts, but that "consciousness of the alphabet . . . [was] a twenty[-]seventh fact" (ibid.). Analogously, in the religious field, James rejected the idealistic thesis that each of us is merely a part of a wider consciousness: "If the absolute makes us by knowing us, how can we exist otherwise than *as* it knows us?" (ibid., 88). This was James's strongest argument against absolute idealism, namely, that it was contrary to our own experience of ourselves as diverse. That is, even if we are only the ideas of the absolute, we *appear* to ourselves differently, and this apparent diversity, even illusion, nonetheless exists. This illusion is not explained simply by ignoring it. On the other hand, admitting that there is diversity but stating that the absolute exists in two respects or under two aspects is also not a sufficient explanation: "What boots it to call the parts and the whole the same body of experience, when in the same breath you have to say that the all 'as such' means one sort of experience and each part 'as such' means another?" (ibid., 92–93). James then sharpens the focus of his attack: it is not so much the *multum-in-parvo* aspect of the absolute that he denies; it is the relegation of this feature of reality to one *part* of it, *together* with the claim that this outlook is completely rational, that is, that there is nothing "preferred" or "empirically appealing." In actuality, he accuses the idealists of being "masked irrationalists"—at least in part—and suggests that candor is better.

Throughout *PU*, one finds indications on James's part that he thought reality was more subtle than any formal system. At the very beginning, he writes, "No philosophy can ever be anything but a summary sketch, a picture of the world in abridgment, a foreshortened birds-eye view of the perspective of events" (*PU*, 9). And again, "[a] philosophy . . . must indeed be true, but that is the least of its requirements" (ibid., 11). Such a metatheoretical outlook has an essential vagueness or open texture to it. The matchup between formal outlook and reality is not a completely neat one. There is room for possibility, for action:

> If we take the whole history of philosophy, the systems reduce themselves to a few main types which, under all the technical verbiage in which the ingenious intellect of man envelops them, are just so many visions, modes of feeling the whole push, and seeing the whole drift of life, forced on one by one's total character and experience, and on the whole *preferred*—there is no other truthful word—as one's best working attitude. (ibid., 14–15)

In statements such as these, James has given advance notice of his metaphysical position. That position maintains that reality is not only broader than the known; it is broader than the knowable. Logic, while necessary, is not a sufficient description of reality. His rejection of the sufficiency of logic is strong and clear:

> For my own part, I have finally found myself compelled to give up the logic, fairly, squarely, and irrevocably. It has an imperishable use in human life, but that use is not to make us theoretically acquainted with the essential nature of reality. . . . Reality, life, experience, concreteness, immediacy, use what word you will, exceeds our logic, overflows and surrounds it. If you like to employ words eulogistically, as most men do, and so encourage confusion, you may say that reality obeys a higher logic, or enjoys a higher rationality. But I think that even eulogistic words should be used rather to distinguish than to commingle meanings, so I prefer bluntly to call reality if not irrational, then at least non-rational in its constitution. (*PU*, 96–97)

James rejected an overly intellectual approach and held that language and concepts per se can only give us aspects of reality.[11] They conceal in the very act of disclosing. James suggests that this overemphasis on intellectualism began as far back as Plato and Socrates, when concepts began to be used "privately as well as positively" (*PU*, 99), that is, not only to define reality but also to exclude the indefinable.

In opposition to all this, he espouses a relational metaphysics. Each moment of experience is related positively and negatively, conjunctively and disjunctively, with a series of others and indirectly with everything else. It is important for our purpose here to recognize James's clear delineation of a metaphysics wherein reality is broader than the known and where this is not simply a temporary problematic: "Thought deals . . . solely with surfaces. It can name the thickness of reality, but it cannot fathom it, and its insufficiency here is essential and permanent, not temporary" (*PU*, 112). And again, "The whole process of life is due to life's violation of our logical axioms" (ibid., 115). What really exists for James "is not things made but things in the making" (ibid., 117). And this process cannot be completely grasped by language, concepts, or thought itself. Each passing moment is more complex than we have realized, more vague and multidimensional than our concepts can pick up. Not only the absolute but also every pulse of experience possesses this common complexity, this vagueness.

## The Metatheoretical Level, the Faith Ladder, and the Will to Believe

So far, James has identified radical empiricism as pluralistic pantheism and asserted that reality is broader than the know-*able*. What happens at this metatheoretical level when one analyzes James's own philosophic position *on its own terms?* Here, the importance of actual possibility clearly emerges. James realized that his own presentation, while it discloses reality, *at the same time* conceals, that is, is only itself a retrospective presentation, through conceptual symbols: "As long as one continues *talking,* intellectualism remains in undisturbed possession of the field. The return to life can't come about by talking. It is an *act;* to make you return to life, I must deafen you to talk. . . . Or I must *point,* point to the mere *that* of life, and you by inner sympathy must fill out the *what* for yourselves" (*PU*, 131).

James's most detailed analysis of his own position occurs at the end of *PU*. In his concluding remarks, he first of all defines God as in some sense finite; the superhuman consciousness, "however vast it may be, has itself an external environment" (*PU*, 140). This, of course, would be demanded by a metaphysic in which reality is broader than the know-*able*. Once this is acknowledged, James argues that the supposed division between a religious rationalism and irreligious empiricism collapses. One can see the divine through the empirical, since each moment of experience is a *"multum-in-parvo"* (ibid., 145), relationally constituted in a pluralistic fashion. God is then in time, in history, etc. (ibid., 144), not above them; *"nothing* real escapes from having an environment" (ibid.).

But having added these final touches, James turns to the issue of possibility as being of great concern. First, he shows that, again, his outlook is *not* one merely of atomism or positivism. Possibility, in terms of a space of operations, does exist:

> Our "multiverse" still makes a "universe"; for every part, tho it may not be in actual or immediate connection, is nevertheless in some possible or mediated connection, with every other part, however remote, through the fact that each part hangs together with its very next neighbors in inextricable interfusion. (*PU,* 146)

And again,

> a thing may be connected by intermediary things, with a thing with which it has no immediate or essential connection. It is thus at all times in many possible connections which are not necessarily actualized at the moment. (ibid.)

Clearly here, again, James is concerned to preserve possibility. That is, the logical possibility of his viewpoint is necessary, even though not sufficient. James says that the "only thing I emphatically insist upon is that it [pluralistic pantheism] is a fully co-ordinate hypothesis with monism. This world *may,* in the last resort, be a block-universe; but on the other hand, it *may* be a universe only strung-along, not rounded in and closed. Reality *may* exist distributively just as it sensibly seems to, after all. On that possibility I do insist" (ibid., 148).

Here James is asserting that his position makes logical sense—that it is not meaningless when compared to monistic idealism, rather that it is a logically possible alternative. But James has also told the reader that the "pragmatic difference between the two systems is . . . a definite one." For an idea to be true pragmatically is for it to be a leading that is worthwhile, to make a difference in our return to the flux of experience, etc. If one asks the question "What difference does it make pragmatically, if one accepts James's outlook, as opposed to monistic idealism?" such a question cannot be answered in terms of logical possibility. The alternate to monistic idealism must be meaningful, that is, logically possible, but that is *not* sufficient.

James shows this by referring to the "faith ladder," the way in which we select one conceptual theory over another:

> A conception of the world arises in you somehow, no matter how. Is it true or not? you ask.

It *might* be true somewhere, you say, for it is not self-contradictory.

It *may* be true, you continue, even here and now.

It is *fit* to be true, it would be *well if it were* true, it *ought* to be true, you presently feel.

It *must* be true, something persuasive in you whispers next; and then—as a final result—It shall be *held for true*, you decide; it *shall be* as if true, for *you*.

And your acting thus may in certain special cases be a means of making it securely true in the end.

Not one step in this process is logical, yet it is the way in which monists and pluralists alike espouse and hold fast to their visions. It is life exceeding logic, it is the practical reason for which the theoretic reason finds arguments after the conclusion is once there. (*PU*, 148)

Here James overstates his case, but only slightly. In analyzing a philosophical conceptualization, he (or the reader) first realizes that it is logically possible. It is not inherently self-contradictory. Such a move is necessary, but by no means sufficient. Analogously, in *Prag*, an idea must have "meaning" in the linguistic sense of "formal significance," but this is not what James was interested in when he asked "What does it *mean* pragmatically, to say that an idea is true?" Here, the putative philosophic system must have formal logical significance, but reality is such that *many* conceptualizations satisfy this demand. As a result, we still have an indeterminacy and a demand for more radical possibility. This is verbalized strongly by James in the language of the contrary-to-fact conditional: "*it would be well if it were true.*" This is clearly actual possibility. In other words, the universe is now so structured that one can say, "Although 'X' (for example, salvation, however defined) is not the case now, it would be the case if each person did his/her level best." Such actualization is clearly more than an empirical statement, in the ordinary sense of empiricism. It describes what is the case in a situation that by definition does not exist. What is most important to note is the fact that the faith ladder, used by James as a final description of his position, is a version of "the will to believe." A decision between the two outlooks must be made that is forced, living, and momentous in nature and then continually reaffirmed. It clearly points out the insufficiency of logic, and it shows that participation, response to a situation, can only take place if actual possibility is affirmed.

In both *ERE* and *PU*, the question of the role of language arises. Is it merely a hindrance or can it serve as a conduit back into the tissue of experience? "Civilization," as Freud said, was rather a mixed blessing. It brought its own achievements in terms of long-term gains over immediate satisfaction, but always at a price. Furthermore, it did not seem possible to return to the past, to "nature" over "nurture," desirable as that might sometimes seem to be.[12] Language, for James, was a bit like civilization was for Freud. That is, he could not live without it, yet it seemed most of the time to sour or to deaden whatever it referred to, to change or ossify reality. Percepts were changed into concepts, oftentimes replacing the "pure experience" he longed to have. This resulted in a certain amount of "discontent" with language. However, not everything James said about language was negative. Furthermore, James goes on using language right up until the very end. So there must, one concludes, be both a good and a bad way to use language.

We explore James's views on language, as well as the availability of pure experience, in the next chapter.

# 7

# "Pure" versus "Impure" Experience

*Examples of Pure Experience*

The question of the availability of pure experience leads directly to the issue of language and to James's ambivalence about language. The question of the availability of pure experience also constitutes the latent content of *Essays in Radical Empiricism (ERE)* and *A Pluralistic Universe (PU)*. Let us take up the issue of language first. There actually exist two different views on language in the Jamesian texts. One of these is disparaging toward language, but the second is more positive in nature.

## The First Position

The first position is the one most readily identified with James, and it is scattered throughout his works. In *The Principles of Psychology (PP)*, for example, he states that

> language works against our perception of the truth. We name our thoughts simply, each after its thing, as if each knew its own thing and nothing else. What each really knows is clearly the thing it is named for, with dimly perhaps a thousand other things.[1]

Here James argues that we take language too much for granted. We all assume that each word has one meaning and that, when the word is used in "x" number of sentences, the meaning is the same. Language so taken, he asserts, is inadequate to the substantive and transitive parts of the stream of consciousness. The sheer inadequacy of language to describe the nuances of the stream is brought out by James in *PP*. Having asserted that relations between things are real, both in the existent order of events and in the stream of consciousness, he continues,

> There is not a conjunction or a preposition, and hardly an adverbial phrase, syntactic form, or inflection of voice, in human speech that does not express some shading or other of relation, which we at some moment actually feel to exist between the larger objects of our thought. If we speak objectively, it is the real relations that appear revealed; if we speak subjectively, it is the stream of consciousness that matches each of them by an inward coloring of its own. In either case the relations are numberless and no existing language is capable of doing justice to all their shades. (*PP*, 1: 238)

Language simply cannot grasp the transitive parts—it either overlooks them, or it substantializes them; in either case, they are not recognized as such. This realization leads James at times to reject language: "Language is the most imperfect and expensive means yet discovered for communicating thought."[2] And again,

> What an awful trade that of professor is—paid to talk, talk, talk! I have seen artists growing pale and sick whilst I talked to them without being able to stop. . . . It would be an awful universe if everything could be converted into words, words, words.[3]

In short, these texts present language as too sluggish. Words, like abstract concepts, are too linear; a sentence turns out to be a set of building blocks. Each part can be separated and does not necessarily affect its neighbor. When James took language "at face value," he found it woefully inadequate: like a statue, it froze the ongoing flux of experience. More importantly, the disjunctions and conjunctions of discourse were considered to be merely neutral logical connectives. As such, language insulates us from dimensions of processive experience, rather than serving as a wedge into the tissue of experience for "pragmatic" purposes. As Graham Bird has noted,

> It was an error due to language which James holds responsible for the faulty atomism of traditional empiricists. There is a natural tendency to cut our stream of consciousness into discrete fragments corresponding to the substantive parts of the stream which we attend to and name. He thinks that such features of language mislead us quite generally, in encouraging us to believe that some thing corresponds to every name and that the absence of a name entails the absence of any discriminable feature. In this general way he echoes Wittgenstein's therapeutic claim that we ascribe to the object what belongs to our method of projection in the language.[4]

However, not everything James wrote about language was negative. He was quite willing to admit that we need labels to find our way about. If one could successfully label an encountered object, it could be subsumed in the right system and its properties immediately known. Indeed, this is the way most of us function: "The only things which we commonly see are those which we pre-perceive . . . which have been labeled for us. If we lost our stock of labels we should be intellectually lost in the midst of the world" (*PP,* 1: 420).

Here James clearly realizes that language cannot be merely "thrown overboard." Language is quite important because of its close connection with conceptualization. It was one means of enabling persons to contain vicariously large amounts of their past experience and, therefore, of enabling them to deal with a novel situation. The only remaining alternative open for James is to construct a different theory of language.

## The Second Position

While no complete theory of language exists in James's work, nonetheless, there does exist a host of "positive" statements that would constitute a good beginning for a linguistic framework. Specifically, James recognized that meanings vary from context to context; he was cognizant of the intentional (or "leading") aspect of discourse; he saw some sentences as essentially directional rather than merely descriptive, and he renounced the view of language as substantive words strung together by neutral logical connectives.

To begin with, James was quite opposed, at times, to the idea of one word having one meaning, irrespective of contextual nuances. He suggests that if "language must . . . influence us, the agglutinative languages, and even Greek and Latin with declensions, would be better guides. Names did not appear in them inalterable, but changed their shape to fit the context in which they lay" (*PP,* 1: 230). James presents the reader with several examples of linguistic "contextual importance" in his works. In *PP,* he says,

> When I use the word *man* in two different sentences, I may have both times exactly the same sound upon my lips and the same picture in my mental eye, but I may mean, and at the very moment of uttering the word and imagining the picture, know that I mean, two entirely different things. Thus when I say: "What a wonderful man Jones is!" I am perfectly aware that I mean by man to exclude Napoleon or Smith. But when I say: "What a wonderful thing Man is!" I am equally well aware that I mean to include not only Jones but Napoleon and Smith as well. (ibid., 1: 446)[5]

This quote develops both the intentional and contextual aspects of language. In either case, a main point seems to be that language is not an objective copy of reality. It does not exist only as an "object"—a much more subtle relationship, an overlapping one between subject, language, and reality, would seem more adequate. There is a sense in which a person structures reality by naming it, by molding it linguistically. This may pose new problems, but it renders inadequate the doctrine that the only purpose of language is the impartial description of events.

Another example, referred to earlier, is the text in *Pragmatism (Prag)* where James tries to articulate the meaning of a statement like "The world is one":

> Granting the oneness to exist, what facts will be different in consequence? . . .
> Many distinct ways in which a oneness predicated of the universe might make
> a difference, come to view . . . (l) . . . [as] one subject of discourse . . . (2) [as]
> continuous . . . (3) . . . Lines of *influence* can be traced by which they hang
> together . . . (4) [in terms of] causal unity . . . (5) [as] generic unity . . . (6) [in
> terms of] one knower. . . ." The world is One," therefore, just so far as we experi-
> ence it to be concatenated. One by as many definite conjunctions as appear. But
> then also *not* One by just as many definite disjunctions as we find. It is neither
> a universe pure and simple nor a multiverse pure and simple. (*Prag*, 65ff.)

The meaning of "one" is not univocal for James, nor is it simply equivocal; there exist rather concatenated "family resemblances" among all of the above meanings of "one," but a reductionism cannot be performed. The only way to ascertain the meaning of "one" is contextually. The emphasis is on richness as opposed to reductionism. Ellen Suckiel has noted this point also:

> For James, as for Wittgenstein later in the century, the meaning of an idea is not sepa-
> rable from the context of its use. To articulate the meaning of an idea is not to rehearse
> a list of other logically equivalent ideas; it is to use that idea as a tool in the context of
> particular concrete problems and concerns. As Wittgenstein was to hold that it is mis-
> guided to search for the meaning of a word outside of that word's own language-game,
> James holds that abstracting concepts out of their particular uses, and treating those ab-
> stractions by themselves as significant, are bound to result in sterility and confusion.[6]

The importance of context is closely aligned with a second aspect of James's positive views on language—the fact that language has a "leading" or "directional" function to perform and, more importantly, that this cannot be divorced from the word, or the sentence, as the case may be: *"names* are just as 'true' or 'false' as definite mental pictures are. They set up similar verification-processes, and lead to fully equivalent practical results" (*Prag*, 213).

James expresses this same view in a slightly different manner in *PP*, where he again notes the leading or directive function of language: "The feeling of an absence is *toto coelo* other than the absence of feeling. . . . Large tracts of human speech are nothing but signs of direction in thought, of which direction we nevertheless have an acutely discriminative sense, though no definite sensorial image plays any part in it whatsoever" (1: 252). Language, then, is directive, and it must be so viewed. Each word, each sentence points beyond itself—it is "leading." James quotes Joseph Joubert approvingly on this subject: "We only know just what we have meant to say, after we have said it" (ibid., 1: 280).

There is, in brief, a vagueness about language, vagueness in the sense of our not knowing what we wanted to say until we have said it. Language does not exist impartially or objectively. We find ourselves involved with it, with the immediate result that we choose certain words without knowing for sure what they mean or, in James's words, where they will lead. As I speak, I am conscious of each word running ahead of itself, feeling at home in the context or not, as the case may be. A word-in-this-context is not the same as a word-in-that-context, but it is not completely different either. There is a richness about words; they can stand for this *or* that *or* the other, and most importantly, the "or's" are not exclusive. Language is rich because it is intense, and vice versa. Like consciousness, it is a sliding focalization, continuous and selective:

> There is about each word the psychic "overtone" of feeling that brings us near
> to a forefelt conclusion. . . . Each word, in . . . a sentence, is felt, not only as a
> word, but as having a *meaning*. The meaning of a word taken thus dynamically
> in a sentence may be quite different from its meaning when taken statically
> or without context. The dynamic meaning is . . . the bare fringe of felt suita-
> bility or unfitness to the context and conclusion. The static meaning, when the
> word is concrete, as "table," "Boston," consists of sensory images awakened;
> when it is abstract, as "criminal legislation," "fallacy," the meaning consists
> of other words aroused, forming the so-called "definition." (*PP*, 1: 264ff.)

Taken statically, then, words have what we might call possible leadings. The basic way to take words, on the other hand, is dynamically, as signs of direction. As such, they point beyond the simple definition or conception toward the situation in which they are used. This "fringe" is conceptually opaque, so we tend to ignore it and to pay attention only to a word and its meaning; or, in other words, we succumb to what James called "vicious intellectualism."[7] To do this is to abstract out of the primary mode of linguistic experience.

From this perspective, each word is a focalization surrounded by a fringe. Going further, not only words but also sentences are focalizations. If language is best articulated as a focus/fringe directional continuum, then the atomistic view of sentences being built up of pieces, nouns and verbs having a value of "1," and connectives being valued at "0," is wrong. The substantive and the transitive parts have to be taken into account. As James says, "The word 'or' names a genuine reality" (*PU*, 324). Again, this point is brought out in *PP:* "We ought to say a feeling of *and*, a feeling of *if*, a feeling of *but*, and a feeling of *by*, quite as readily as we say a feeling of blue or a feeling of cold" (1: 275).

Finally, in *ERE*, James states,

> Prepositions, copulas, and conjunctions, "is," "isn't," "then," "before," "in," "on," "beside," "between," "next," "like," "unlike," "as," "but," flower out of the stream of pure experience, the stream of concretes or the sensational stream, as naturally as nouns and adjectives do, and they melt into it again as fluidly when we apply them to a new portion of the stream. (95)

In brief, for James, all the sections of a sentence are real, as all the sections of consciousness were; furthermore, they are not really separate sections at all:

> But the *object* of your thought is really its entire content or deliverance, neither more nor less. It is a vicious use of speech to take out a substantive kernel from its content and call that its object; and it is an equally vicious use of speech to add a substantive kernel not articulately included in its content, and to call that its object. (*PP*, 1: 265)

The entire content includes the intention and the leading or directional aspect of the sentence. It also includes both substantive and transitive parts of discourse.

In sum, language, like life, is ongoing, unfinished; as such, it has a "vagueness" about it. James occasionally senses this and at times tries to articulate it. On the other hand, language is often taken (even by James) as being chopped up, static, and fixed. When James does take language in this second way, he is extremely critical of its inadequacy to do justice to the richness and intensity of experience. But there are times when the positive tone prevails, and we receive "sketches" of a much more dynamic view of language. In addition, one must always keep in mind the fact that James himself is using language and, for the most part, is quite conscious of this. Language is for him a continuation of the battle of life "felt as a real fight"; in addition, the language of James's text exists as a provocation to the reader.[8]

## Impure Experience and "Exemplars" of Pure Experience

Perhaps we can make some progress toward pure experience and its availability or nonavailability by contrasting it with "impure" experience, that is, experience that is degenerate, sullied, fallen. *Funk and Wagnalls New Practical Standard Diction-*

*ary* (1956) defines *impure* as, among other things, "containing some foreign substance"; "adulterated"; "unchaste"; as "containing foreign idioms or grammatical blemishes"; as "unfit for religious use"; as "unhallowed"; etc. What would render experience "foreign," "barbaroi," or barbarian? What is a grammatical blemish? Is experience infected by language? How does language blemish? Does language *have* to blemish? Are all blemishes grammatical? Do we, you and I, live in a world of relatively impure experience? Is pure experience only for newborn babes? And for people under anesthesia? Can we become childlike? Do we *want* to become childlike? To anesthetize is to "go under." Is James, unintentionally glossing Friedrich Nietzsche, calling for this? Going further, this "pure" state is not always perfectly safe. "The environment," James warns, "kills as well as sustains us"—and our verbal fixations, sullied as they are, let us "know what is in the wind for us and get ready to react in time" (*ERE*, 47). "In time"—that is, in flux. In time—and "on time." We seem to need to redescend into pure experience, at least temporarily—dangerous, wild and "game-flavored"[9] as that may be. Language, used as directional rather than merely descriptive, can be quite helpful here.

A complete recovery of pure experience is not feasible, and there is something poignant about this realization. However, partial "escapes" are possible. Examples of such moments would include but not be limited to the following: (1) nature (for example, James's mountain-walking journeys in the Adirondacks); (2) art (such as becoming a proficient dancer in the Martha Graham dance troupe); (3) sport (for example, having a night where one is "simply unconscious" in successful scoring); and (4) religion, especially mysticism.

In *The Varieties of Religious Experience (VRE)* as is noted in chapter 4 above, it was suggested that the best way to acquire an awareness of pure experience was to employ the notion of an "exemplar" or "crude analogy" as that term is applied by Thomas Kuhn. Going further, an example of this was provided, namely, focusing on the mystical experience as an exemplar of pure experience. James himself never had a mystical experience, yet he was very "sympathetic" to those who claimed to have had them. Going further, he uses language in a very sympathetic way, so as to lead the reader up to the edge of having a mystical experience. There exist other possible exemplars of pure experience. These include aesthetic experience, the experience of nature while hiking, and selected moments while participating in a sport. Let us look at each of these briefly.

The first connection, namely, the aesthetic, is an easy one to make. James himself in *VRE* turns to music as a conduit to mystical experiences, claiming that "In mystical literature such self-contradictory phrases as 'dazzling obscurity,' 'whispering silence,' 'teeming desert,' are continually met with. They prove that not conceptual speech, but music rather, is the element through which we are best spoken to by mystical truth. Many mystical scriptures are indeed little more than musical compositions."[10]And again, "music gives us ontological messages which non-musical criticism is unable to contradict, though it may laugh at our foolishness in minding them" (*VRE*, 334). Commenting on these texts, Ellen Suckiel asserts that "James is not suggesting that mystical experience is non-cognitive. Rather, he is invoking a notion of understanding which is more primary than propositional understanding."[11] She argues that there is a wide array of knowledge that is not propositional in nature: "The gymnast, dancer, or diver develops a kinesthetic self-awareness, and through experience and attention to that experience has a sense, not reducible to a set of propositions, of the appropriate timing and effort required for such maneuvers."[12] A similar point is made by Jessica Pierce, who utilizes the work of the Martha Graham dance troupe as a form of pure experience: "The development of pure experience parallels the discipline of art, in that each essentially requires the will to unify the artist and medium to the point where they are one and the same. As artists mature in their art, and directly experience their own consciousness, there will be no discrimination between themselves and the medium or object. For example, the Graham repertoire (Martha Graham's modern dance) cannot be performed by only learning a sequence of movements, no matter how brilliantly the dancers master the technical difficulties—and they are considerable."[13] There is a sense in which one becomes "unconscious," so to speak: "Pure experience exists when that which was first *conscious* for the artist becomes *unconscious* and he or she and their medium are one."[14] This is a phenomenon asserted by both James and Nishida Kitaro, the Japanese philosopher whose book *An Inquiry into the Good* was heavily influenced by James's views on "pure experience." Nishida gives as two examples of pure experience "a climber's determined ascent of a cliff and a musician's performance of a piece that has been mastered through practice."[15] For Nishida, too, "as one matures in art, that which at first was conscious becomes unconscious."[16]

The reference to the Martha Graham dance troupe and the physical demands necessary to achieve a (relatively) pure experience can serve as an entry point into a third area of possible pure experience, namely, the world of sport. When someone has a particularly good night as a player, as in, say, basketball, we oftentimes say that he or she is "unconscious." This is not literally true—just as it was not so for mystical experiences. Rather what it connotes is that one has become so good, so seamless in the performance of one's task, scoring baskets or performing a demanding choreography, that it seems effortless. Of course, nothing was effortless when one first joined the troupe or took one's first shots on the basketball court.

The reference made by Nishida to climbing a cliff can serve as a final example or "exemplar" of pure experience, namely, one's communion with nature. In 1875, James started going to Keene Valley in the Adirondacks for summer respites. He thought that the place, with its fragrant woods and mountain streams, was extremely beautiful. "When not mountain climbing," his biographer Linda Simon tells us, "James spent hours reading, usually fifty pages a day. He had a special spot where he secluded himself with a book: a ledge overlooking the Ausable River, where he would lie sheltered by trees on a bed of pine needles."[17] James identified mountain climbing with the "strenuous life"—one that required effort and "manliness." It could also be dangerous. In 1899, James went for an extended hike to the top of rugged Mount Marcy, but he got lost, took the wrong road, and barely managed to wander into camp at 10:15 PM, exhausted and frightened. He had restrained his heart—already injured a year earlier. This was something from which he never fully recovered.[18] In sum, nature remained, at least at times and in certain places, "wild, game flavored as a hawk's wing."

These exemplars provide some indication as to what a more "democratic" and less exclusive approach to pure experience might look like. They are examples only, essentially incomplete and partial—but nonetheless informative. They serve as illustrations of the type of universe James believed in—one that was unfinished, challenging, and vague. As such, it was a universe that demanded that we exercise the will to believe.

Inviting as such a challenge might be, there are some for whom this approach is insufficient or misleading or too demanding. In the next chapter, we turn to the major challenges mounted against "the will to believe."

# 8

# Challenges to
# "The Will to Believe"

Challenges to "The Will to Believe" come from two sides, the Right and the Left. The "manifest" challenge comes from the Right and has traditionally been associated with the critique of A. J. Ayer and other positivists. It suggests that James was not as logically consistent as he should have been and that he should have been clearer. Ayer's critique is forcefully stated in *The Origins of Pragmatism*. It stems from his earlier work *Language, Truth and Logic*. The more "latent" attack comes from the Left, and it suggests that the will to believe may be more difficult to carry out than James admits.

## The Critique of A. J. Ayer

In *Language, Truth and Logic,* Ayer offers a general theory of meaning that can be summed up in a few general propositions.[1] First, if you know something, you can say it; the "ineffable" has no place here. Second, statements "said" are either meaningful or meaningless, and these can be clearly distinguished. Third, a meaningful statement is one capable of being classified as "true" or "false." Fourth, there are only two types of meaningful statements, tautologies and empirically verifiable propositions. (It is the latter that Ayer is most concerned with.) Finally, any statement not classifiable as either tautological or verifiable is "gibberish," that is, meaningless. These include religious statements, aesthetic statements, ethical statements, metaphysical statements, etc. These are all termed "emotive utterances" and are expressions of feeling—as opposed to meaningful statements. As Ayer reads James, these distinctions are present in his writing but not drawn out precisely enough. For James, according to Ayer,

> The criteria by which we have to assess a belief which relates to a matter of empirical fact are different from those which apply to a belief which is concerned only with relations between ideas and these are different again from the criteria which apply to beliefs whose function is to satisfy our moral and emotional requirements. These distinctions are implicit in James's writing but he does not draw attention to them.[2]

In opposition, one might argue that James was at pains to show that these distinctions are not found at the primary level of experience.

Ayer continues his critique by suggesting that James's dislike of logic applied only to a certain domain. It was "policed," so to speak: "James's tendency to look askance at logic becomes easier to understand when it is remembered that the logic with which he was principally confronted was the logic of Hegel" (*The Origins of Pragmatism*, 176). Ayer correctly notes that what James finds morally shocking in Hegelianism is its pretense that such experiences as pain and evil are not real. In actuality, Ayer seems to pass over James's dissatisfaction with logic per se— attributing it to a local, historical figure, namely, G. W. F. Hegel. Ayer admits that James is similar to Henri Bergson and to existentialism, but having admitted it, he proceeds to ignore it for the rest of the book:

> Whatever problems it may encounter we shall not be likely to find that the line of "giving up logic" on the ground that reality in its experienced concreteness "exceeds, overflows and surrounds it" provides the solution to them. In spite of the respect for hard fact which governs all his philosophizing, I doubt indeed that James would have made this concession to irrationalism if his running fight with the Hegelians had not left him with the mistaken feeling that there was an unbridgeable gulf between the static world of intellectual concepts, in which for all the apparent agitation of their dialectic the Hegelians complacently dwell, and the dynamic flux of experience in which ordinary men move and have their being. (*The Origins of Pragmatism*, 179)

Ayer also believes that "pure experience" should be accepted merely as a heuristic device, that is, as an upper-case limit. While admitting that James probably did claim that pure experience is all that there is, Ayer holds that "interpreted in this way, the thesis is very dubious indeed. To begin with, it is not clear what a claim of this kind amounts to, outside the framework of a given system" (*The Origins of Pragmatism*, 318). With this strong emphasis on meaning, Ayer asserts that

> It may well be that the best course is to take no ontological decisions at all. If we
> adopt this policy, we shall construct questions about the reality of different sorts
> of objects only as asking whether the statements which figure in different types of
> theory are true. . . . if we are able to determine which statements at each of these
> levels are true and how statements of different kinds are related to each other,
> there are no matters of truth or falsehood left to be decided. . . . In dissenting from
> James on this aspect of his thesis that experience is the primal stuff of the world,
> I have taken a pragmatic view of ontology. (*The Origins of Pragmatism*, 322–23)

Whatever the merits of this outlook on its own grounds, James would surely have found it unacceptable. First, it implies the traditional positivist clear distinction between the meaningful and the meaningless; and, indeed, Ayer in other places divides James's writings into moral-theological on the one hand and epistemological on the other.[3] But in *Pragmatism (Prag)*, James specifically rejected such a dichotomy; he viewed his new method as a mediator between the tough minded and the tender minded.[4] Hence, Graham Bird is correct in his assertion that Ayer's "account is misleading in its suggestion that James drew a totally sharp distinction between moral and scientific beliefs. For this overlooks the fact that James regarded emotional satisfaction as important even in the scientific case."[5] Furthermore, James's views on language indicate a contextualist position where the line between meaningful and meaningless cannot be clearly drawn.

A second aspect of James's position, which would argue strongly against Ayer's interpretation, is his critique of "vicious intellectualism."[6] Here James clearly rejects the reduction or reification of meaning to the stage where the meaning of meaning is constituted by formal semantics. As we have seen, in James's positive linguistic views, "meaning" included intention (what I want or need) and effect (the practical results of a given idea or statement). Usually he is criticized for not distinguishing them clearly, but it may well be the case that James believed that no such distinction could be made, at least in any complete sense.

For these reasons, James would not accept the notion that pure experience had meaning only insofar as it was considered true or false within the confines of some specific linguistic system. More and more, James became suspicious of language, especially in its most reified form—logic. So, while it is necessary to point out that "pure experience" is not grounded on an apodictic foundation, it is also necessary to reject the interpretation of pure experience as merely a convenient device, necessary to posit but then eminently forgettable.

We turn now to critiques stemming from the Left and coming from Fyodor Dostoevsky and Franz Kafka.

## Notes from the Underground

Dostoevsky's underground man is very worried about being predictable when he chooses. Dostoevsky wrote the text in opposition to one written by Nikolai Chernyshevsky, titled *What Is to Be Done?* In this text, moral choices about, for example, whether a young woman should marry an older but wealthy man were made in terms of scientific calculation, that is, a form of utilitarianism. In opposition, the underground man says sometimes it is better to say that two plus two is five rather than four. Sometimes it is better not to accept that we are descended from apes, even though it is incontrovertible, etc. The only way the underground man can see to maintain his freedom is to be "spiteful." He defines a human being as someone who stands on his hind legs and is spiteful. The underground man is dancing as fast as he can. He is free, but at a terrible price. Spite remains his only way of "communicating" both with Lisa, the main female character in the story, and with you, the reader. The underground man or woman is one step away from exhaustion or surrender—surrender to the argument of the Grand Inquisitor, who has made the people happy by taking away their freedom. He has given them "miracle, mystery, and authority," in short, certainty. The underground man barely manages to maintain his spite, snarling at the reader that she is already "dead" as she "abstractly" reads the last page of the story.

For James, one chooses not for spiteful but for "passionate" or "sentimental" reasons. The challenge to James, which parallels the temptation offered by the Grand Inquisitor, comes from his colleague Josiah Royce. Like the Grand Inquisitor, Royce initially seems to say that the will to believe asks too much of us. He argues that "life has its un-heroic days."[7] Royce, in *The Religious Aspect of Philosophy,* offers certainty in the form of an argument for the existence of God based on the existence of human error. By the time Royce published *The Philosophy of Loyalty,* his position has evolved into one of more than "mere postulates," that is, it is one of "commitment," albeit to something eternal and certain. Royce defines "loyalty" as "the will to believe in something eternal, and to express that belief in the practical life of a human being."[8] Earlier in this text, he had argued, in a very Jamesian fashion, for the necessity of choosing among causes, and not playing the role of Hamlet: "Decide, knowingly if you can, ignorantly if you must, but in any case decide, and have no fear" ("Loyalty and Religion," 312). Royce sees his position here as quite analogous to that offered by his colleague James in "The Will to Believe." Perhaps anticipating a criticism, Royce hastens to say that this "is no sort of 'moral holiday'" (ibid., 341). Whether Royce has shifted paradigms radically in these two texts may be left for another time. But his statement that we all have "un-heroic days," that is, ones where we not only will not but, rather, cannot cope, requires attention.

It would be hard to find a better portrait of a bad day than that provided by Franz Kafka in his novel *The Trial*.

## The Trial

In Kafka's *The Trial*, we are presented with a text that allows for, and even demands, multiple interpretations of an incommensurate nature. At the very beginning, the hero (or anti-hero), Joseph K., rings a bell, and his trial commences. Does he put himself on trial, or is he brought to the trial by the law? He says later on in the text that the "guilt lies with the organization," but this statement could be merely a diversion, that is, a form of repression. Is K. a representative of nineteenth-century bourgeois capitalism, or does he transcend this sociopolitical situation? But there is also some evidence for a more psychological interpretation of the novel, one suggesting that K. is repressing some more acontextual truth or necessity, that is, that the alienation is fundamental to human nature at large. At the very beginning, he encounters two warders; one of them is named "Franz" (not coincidentally). As K. brushes by him, that is, as K. "crosses the threshold," he encounters the second warder, reading a book, who tells him that the two warders "stand closer to him than any other people in the world"; he also says that Franz should have told him to stay in his room. The two warders show up later in the lumber room of the bank, where they are about to receive a whipping. In "real life," banks do not have lumber rooms, but *rumplekammer* in German carries with it the connotation of dead text and dry ink wells, that is, perhaps the semi-repressed image of Kafka as a failed writer—one who could not create.

From an existential perspective, K. is guilty of "bad faith," of not assuming the upright posture, of trying to become "thing-like," an *en soi*. Twice in the novel, he is treated as an object and seems to find some satisfaction or at least relief in this. Indeed, at the end of the novel, he *is* almost a thing, almost, but not quite, a piece of matter being carried to the quarry by his warders. Yet, even here, closure is not to be had, as Kafka tells the reader, on the last line of the text, that "the shame of it must outlive him,"[9] that is, that, even at the end, there is *not* an end. K. will live on ignominiously, "like a dog," in the reader/author's mind.

There is also a religious interpretation of the novel, ending with the famous parable of the doorkeeper, where a man from the country approaches and tries to enter a door being guarded by a doorkeeper. He is told he cannot do so, at least not at the present moment, and winds up spending his entire life waiting at the side of the door and not trying to push through. At the end, when he is about to expire, he asks the doorkeeper why no one else has ever shown up at the door and is told that the door was only for him and that it is now about to be shut. The parable, like the text, is open to multiple interpretations. Did the doorkeeper lie to the man? Or only tell him the truth when asked? Can he really shut the door, etc.? Joseph K.'s activity, or lack thereof in the text, raises the religious issue of the covenant of grace vis-à-vis the covenant of works. Can one do anything about one's "sinful" condition, or should one rather merely accept it on "blind," that is, not "informed" faith? There is a real question in Kafka's text as to whether the attempt to investigate the situation is *itself* a form of pride or hubris. Or is it rather the case that K.'s investigation is noteworthy and commendable, but that his refusal to act without certainty, that is, to engage in the "will to believe," is grounds for criticism? Kafka might reply that Joseph K. was *incapable* of acting otherwise than he did, that he was not quite up to being human. It was not, in short, that K. has existentially or religiously lapsed from a previous state or, if so, that he could do anything about it. He was more "like a dog," that is, prehuman or posthuman.

We are left then with the metaphor of the mountain pass confronting the parable of the doorkeeper. James says that you cannot do *nothing*, that is, wait by the door, not try to get down the mountain in the snowstorm. Kafka says do not move until you have a clear view, not just a glimpse. When does an obstructed view become a glimpse? This, we should note, is a "vague" question, for it admits of no precise answer—like the sorites question: "After the addition of which particular grain of sand does a pile become a heap"?

Hilary Putnam has argued that "The Will to Believe" is akin to the situation faced by Pierre in Jean-Paul Sartre's "Existentialism and Humanism." This is not, in other words, a mere matter of calculating the consequences and then choosing on this basis.[10] While Putnam is right to compare Sartre to James, the issue of *both* Sartre and James confronting Kafka's Joseph K. remains, and this also cannot be solved by logical argument. Joseph K. could be interpreted as someone in "bad faith," that is, as someone who refuses to exercise the will to believe. He wants certainty, a.k.a. definite acquittal, and refuses to do anything until it is attained. Since it never arrives, K. does nothing throughout the duration of the novel. But, on another level, K. is unable, not unwilling, to exercise the will to believe. The intimation of the novel is that K. did nothing but also that, if he did try, he would have failed in his attempt. K. was not unwilling to take the knife at the end and commit suicide; he was unable to do so.

The picture provided to us in *The Trial* is precisely akin to that presented by James in "The Sentiment of Rationality," and it is one James says that we, as humans, will not accept. It is totally pessimistic, and it gives us no role to play. The argument between James and Kafka is not one that can be solved. There are no crucial experiments to be set up to prove that one is right and the other wrong. Both can, to a degree, appeal to experience. Kafka may be too pessimistic, James too romantic. James might be able to claim that Joseph K. is not the rule, that is, is not everyman or everywoman. Kafka might respond by saying that James's Promethean self is overly romantic, that is, is the exception to the rule, rather than the rule itself, perhaps representative of the Grand Inquisitor, but not of humankind in general. James would admit that the Clifford-like character named Joseph K. cannot be "proven" wrong or inadequate in character development. (W. K. Clifford was James's major protagonist in "The Will to Believe," who upheld the thesis that one should never believe in anything in the absence of sufficient evidence.) James can only point to the ambiguity or vagueness of the situation and suggest to us, the readers, that at a metalevel the situation *itself* is forced, living and momentous, thereby requiring us to choose, which, of course, is precisely what Joseph K. either will not or cannot do. Once again, the will to believe is not a problem to be solved. It is a stance, a position that, perhaps, has to be continually reaffirmed. It is not a matter of believing *that*, but rather a matter of believing *in*, as D. Micah Hester and Michael Talisse have noted in their volume *On James*.[11] Or, in Jamesian terms, it is "life exceeding logic."

James did not seem to feel that he had to go as far as Dostoevsky, that is, to affirm "spitefulness" in order to preserve freedom. But he did appear to feel that he had to go further than John Dewey, who seemed, at least sometimes, to believe that every event was at least potentially problematic, that is, capable of being solved, even if the solution was not of a permanent or certain nature. The Jamesian self is both sentimental and strenuous but also frail and fallible; the Dostoevsky self is a spiteful one, with two worries. First, Dostoevsky worries that true freedom will be undermined by a degenerate form or a variation of itself, namely, probability or calculation. Second, the strong case that Dostoevsky made for the position of the Grand Inquisitor has led many to believe that Dostoevsky himself agreed that most people just cannot bear freedom. The self portrayed for us by Kafka is a "shameful" self. Joseph K. is manipulative and very ad hoc in dealing with people in specific situations. He wants certainty, that is, definite acquittal, but fails to find it because, in the tortured logic of Kafka's world, the very asking of the question takes away salvation.

It is instructive to note that the three texts—"The Will to Believe," *Notes from the Underground,* and *The Trial*—all end with the subject of death and the attitude we have, or should have, toward it. Joseph K. dies like a dog, that is, at a sub-human but sentient level. He is either unwilling or, more probably, unable to take the knife passed back and forth over him by his warders. The underground man suggests that his readers are already half-dead "cripples" who cannot stand real life: "We are still born . . . [and] are developing a taste for it."[12] For James, "[w]e stand on a mountain pass in the midst of whirling snow and blinding mist, through which we get glimpses now and then of paths which may be deceptive," etc., etc. "What must we do? 'Be strong and of a good courage.' Act for the best, hope for the best, and take what comes. . . . If death ends all, we cannot meet death better."[13] Certainty is something Joseph K. wants; he just does not get it. The underground man is resisting with all his might, but he might not make it. As Robert Lord has noted, *Notes from the Underground* "anticipates Kafka."[14] James's "Promethean self" is perhaps better off. But we should remember James's own vulnerability to melancholia and depression—witness his temptation to suicide and his veiled reference to the epileptic figure who was, in fact, himself in *The Varieties of Religious Experience.*[15] The James scholar John McDermott admonishes us to keep this in mind: "If it can be said that James assented to 'The Will to Believe' until the end, we must caution that it was a belief always shot through with irresolution and doubt. Behind the constant cadences of a rich and future-oriented prose, there lurked a well-controlled but omnipresent sense of despair."[16] Or, as Phil Oliver has noted in *"Springs of Delight,"* James's "bootstrapping" approach to depression and suicide indicates that this was not a "problem" for him to solve, once and for all.[17]

This can be put differently by saying that, while martial metaphors may be necessary for James, they are not completely sufficient. That is, it is not a matter of deciding, on a onetime basis, to take life aggressively and, hence, solve the issue by exercising the will to believe; for some times we will fail to do so. While James might urge us to inculcate the "habit" of exercising the will to believe, we must recognize that we are, as Nietzsche might say, "human all too human" and, therefore, will sometimes fail to do so. But we will not necessarily fail all the time, Kafka to the contrary. Nor must we necessarily pay the dreadfully high price for it, as portrayed by Dostoevsky.

The will to believe is a cardinal element in the Jamesian corpus. It appears, in one version or another, at least four times. It describes for us, in Deweyan terms, a uniquely qualified indeterminate situation but one that is not "problematic" in nature. The major difference between tragedy and the will to believe is that one perspective is forward-looking and the other is retrospective in nature. This difference, while very important, should not be allowed to efface what they have in common; both are modes of being that are other than "problematic" in nature.

In sum, there is something nonproblematic, if not tragic, present in James that is not present, or at least not *as* present, in Dewey. The worlds of Dostoevsky or of Kafka would indeed be very peripheral to Dewey's vision—profound as it was. But the worlds of Kafka and Dostoevsky would be closer to that of James, at least insofar as all three had a "problem with problems." Kafka would indeed like his character Joseph K. to be able to solve the problem of salvation, but he posed the problem in such a fashion as to perpetuate its continual existence. It is the very asking of the question "What must I do to be saved?" that constituted the problem and that simultaneously prevents it from being solved. If Dostoevsky does indeed anticipate Kafka, we may view the realm of the Grand Inquisitor in *The Brothers Karamazov* as that of a problem solved, once and for all, that is, certainty attained, except for the few hundred thousand who know the awful truth. Joseph K. wants certainty, a.k.a. definite acquittal, and not merely ostensive acquittal (read "probability") but does not get it. The underground man is only one step away from "heaven on earth," that is, certainty, and the discovery that there is a "genetic explanation" for his spite, as a form of recumbent DNA.

James's self is neither the shameful self left at the end of *The Trial* nor the spiteful self flailing away at the end of *Notes from the Underground*. But neither is he exclusively the Promethean self for whom everything might be viewed as a problem to be solved, a sort of Nietzschean camel. The Jamesian sentimental or passionate self would reject the paradigm offered by Kafka as inaccurate or at least incomplete; that is, not everything goes wrong with one's life all at once, all the time. Most of the time, we "solve" matters, via a marriage function, by trying for a minimum of jolt and a maximum of continuity, as James says in *Prag*.[18] But sometimes things do go wrong in a cataclysmic fashion; the options are forced and exclusionary in nature. Perhaps the paradigms become incompatible and not just incommensurate. The Jamesian self would also reject the picture offered by Dostoevsky, the one offering spite as the only or the most important emotion, though agreeing on the importance of emotion. You do need to be idiosyncratic, for James, to select among forced options for nonpredictable reasons, but you do not have to be spiteful to do so. You can admit that your errors are not such serious things, as he does in "The Will to Believe." On the other hand, all is not play; you have the right to believe, to risk your own life for some particular goal, option, or cause.

Is this enough? Has it gotten harder to exercise the will to believe since James wrote the article? Perhaps it just gets harder for each individual as he or she ages. James himself kept trying to exercise the will to believe through one crisis after another throughout his life—and it did get harder to keep on "dancing." But he did dance, that is, write, his own form of exercising the will to believe, up until the very end. Perhaps this is his answer to Kafka and Dostoevsky—if "answer" is the correct term. If so, it may have been a very "pragmatic" one. For, truly, the proof of the pudding is in the eating or, in this case, in the writing.

John McDermott once wrote, "I now believe, shakily, insecurely, and barely, that life is worth living."[19] Perhaps this is the only way to exercise "the will to believe"—shakily, insecurely, and barely. If so, it may be easier to see that, for James, not everything is a problem. If James reminds us of how important it is to highlight the importance of the uncertain, or the vague, Dostoevsky and Kafka remind us of how difficult it oftentimes is to do so.

James's answer to Dostoevsky and Kafka is twofold: the will to believe and pluralism, that is, a fat and multifarious context. True, there are spiteful moments and also Kafkaesque situations. But there are also prospective will-to-believe moments, as well as Deweyan problematic moments subject to inquiry. Pluralism allows us to accept the tragic as a subset of reality, while offering alternatives. But while tragic situations cannot be "solved," they can perhaps be countered by offering alternative options. The tragic experience should not be explained away, but neither should it be taken as indicative of experience in general. The same can, and should, be said concerning the attribution of the term *problematic* to experience. That is, some moments are not just potential problems or puzzles waiting to be solved. One of these concerns the tragic. But another concerns the "will to believe."

In our conclusion, we return to the text of *Prag* for a final review—this time focusing on the manifest image found in the internal lectures dealing with pragmatism as a method, vis-à-vis the beginning and ending lectures that deal with pragmatism and death.

# Conclusion

*Pragmatism, Death, and "The Will to Believe"*

As was seen in the previous chapters, the importance of the individual was a topic central to James's thought. This chapter will focus on how individuals comport themselves at the end of life insofar as this can be gleaned from the text of *Pragmatism (Prag)* itself. My analysis begins with an observation, perhaps with a detour of sorts. The "manifest content" of *Prag* concerns its image as a method and as a theory of truth. Both of these are important. However, there is also a more "latent" content to *Prag*. The method and the theory of truth are "situated" in a more nebulous "context." That context can be found in the first and last lectures of the text. Both of these turn to the subject of "death" as an important theme with which pragmatism must deal. "Dealing," it may be noted, does not necessarily mean "solving." Dealing may have to do with affirming, even if not wholly accepting or, alternatively, declaring "tragic" and incomprehensible. Any view of pragmatism as a method or "problem solver" can be rejected or at least significantly limited in power and scope by noting domains where and how it does and does not apply. In sum, this concluding chapter will focus on death (suicide) and tragedy, as these are found in *Prag*. These seem not to be "solvable" via the pragmatic method because they are not problems to begin with. They may be "resolvable," that is, appropriated or rejected, but that entails utilization of "the will to believe." Thus, we return to the theme brought forth at the outset of this volume on James, namely, the pervasiveness of "the will to believe" in his thought.

## The Beginning: Pragmatism and Death

*Prag* begins with two examples about death. The two examples come from a pamphlet titled "Human Submission" by the anarchist Morrison Swift, who was a little extreme for James's tastes, but with whom he nonetheless sympathized a great deal. In one pamphlet, John Corcoran, an unemployed clerk, "ended his life by drinking carbolic acid."[1] He had found work as a snow-shoveler but was too weak from illness to sustain the pace after one hour. On returning home, he found that his wife and children had no food and that he had been dispossessed. He ingested the poison the following day. James selected as a second example from Morrison a Cleveland worker who kills his children and himself. James agrees with Morrison that this type of case or situation discloses reality in all its elemental rawness and that it cannot be explained by being explained *away*. This had oftentimes been the project of religion and of religious idealism and its many treatises on God, Love, and Being.[2]

But more than the rationalizations of religious idealism is at fault here. James opened the lectures on *Prag* by "inventing the problematic" or outlining "the present dilemma in philosophy." He divided the world of philosophy into two camps, the "tough-minded" and the "tender-minded," admitting that the division was rather oversimplistic in nature and that he has great difficulty in attributing "freedom" to either camp. He initially lists it under the tender minded but seems to remove it shortly thereafter, saying that tender-minded rationalism believes in systems and that systems are closed. James finds it difficult to accept the findings of either camp exclusively. The tender minded are too ethereal and abstract, the tough minded too unromantic, even if they do seem to deal with this world. Neither camp is very "intimate" with life. The two examples from Morrison's text are offered as examples from the latter, that is, of real experience with which, thus far at least, the abstract written treatises of philosophers had been *unwilling* or *unable* to deal.

The difference here is an important one. Have philosophers heretofore chosen to emphasize the abstract over the concrete? To replace and not reflect life as it is actually lived? Does language per se, or logic per se, or "thinking" per se necessarily do this? Or, on a deeper level, is it just the case that "humankind cannot stand very much reality?" If the first alternative is the case, then the situation can still be salvaged. And indeed, James, in this first lecture, throws his philosophical hat in the ring, saying, "I offer the oddly-named thing pragmatism as a philosophy that can satisfy both kinds of demand [tough minded and tender minded]" (*Prag,*

23). But even if salvageable, two important caveats are still in order. First, James stated at the very beginning of the first lecture that "[t]he history of philosophy is to a great extent that of a certain clash of human temperaments" (ibid., 11). This indicates, on a self-reflexive level, that pragmatism involves an attitude or a stance toward reality, rather than a solving of the latter as if it were a problem.

Second, accounts are interpretations, more akin to metaphors than descriptions, and limited in scope. This could be due to the nature of language or to the nature of reality itself. Even if an account is possible, there are good and bad accounts—or "fat" accounts and "thin" accounts: "An outline in itself is meagre, truly, but it does not necessarily suggest a meagre thing. It is the essential meagreness of *what is suggested* by the usual rationalistic philosophies that moves empiricists to their gesture of rejection" (*Prag,* 25). Accounts, then, due to the very nature of language itself, can provide only limited access to reality. In one sense of the term, empiricism is more concrete than rationalist religious systems. But in another sense, both religion and science have explained reality, or at least some types of reality, by explaining it *away.* Accounts are limited, but some are more "intimate" with life than others. To be successful, James's account must be more than merely descriptive; it must be "directive," pointing beyond itself toward a return to life, a "leading that is worth while," rather than just a static correspondence. And it must deal with life in its "concreteness," not explain the concreteness away.

Let us return to our two examples from Morrison and to James's offering of pragmatism as a mediator. Can pragmatism deal with the two deaths given in the text? And does "deal with" mean "explain" or "make meaningful"? Or does it rather mean appropriate, make one's own, even if not completely comprehensible? Both deaths are, in a sense, senseless, that is, unnecessary, avoidable. The death of the clerk and that of the Cleveland workman might be explained, or accounted for, in terms of an unjust socioeconomic system. Altering the system would, arguably, dissolve the perceived need to commit suicide out of despair. In other words, if the situation is perceived as a "problem" in Deweyan terms,[3] then a proposed solution can be offered. Both anarchism and Marxism, in all their variations, might be put forth as potential competing paradigms to solve it. Some "explanations" might be better than others, pragmatically speaking, for example, Marxism as opposed to Leibnizian rationalism, because it offers an actual solution to a concrete problem in *this* world—as opposed to a rationalization of the status quo.

But if the specific examples of death alluded to here can be accounted for in one respect, death per se cannot. That is, individual personal deaths cannot be rendered "acceptable" just because they can be understood "in the long run," as part of an ongoing evolutionary process. If this is so, every individual death is in some sense "tragic."[4] A situation is tragic not merely because good is pitted against good but rather because it remains in some sense "unmediated." There are "dregs" left behind, so to speak. As Kathleen Higgins puts it, "the kind of suffering from which tragedy draws its material is not remedied by thinking the situation through."[5] However, James does flirt with "thinking the situation of death through" in *Prag*. As we will see, he offers a wedding, a mediation, a way of interpreting tragedy as provisional in nature when he discusses "spiritualism" versus "materialism." But ultimately he does *not* explain tragedy by explaining it *away*.

James never returns to the two suicides offered as "exemplars"[6] of what we need to deal with in the real world. But he does offer pragmatism as a mediator, and, at the end, he does offer meliorism as a viable approach to the issue of salvation. However, sometimes mediation does not work, resulting in "forced" choices rather than marriage. Going further, James's offering of meliorism was quickly tempered, if not rescinded, as he wondered, "[m]ay not the claims of tender-mindedness go too far?" (*Prag*, 141). The self that emerges from this compromise is more fragile and tragic than just Promethean in nature. James realizes that meliorism is not just a position to be proved intellectually, but rather that it needs to be passionately affirmed, even in the face of uncertainty. Furthermore, that affirmation must be continuously renewed—and we will not be equally successful in doing so each and every time. Finally, while meliorism on the surface remains a positive outlook, there remains, just beneath the surface, the threat that it may ask too much of us.

We should read *Prag* keeping in mind that James himself seriously contemplated suicide during the period 1868–1870 and that, ultimately, he did *not* solve the issue as a methodological problem but rather "got over it" by exercising the "will to believe." James's thoughts of suicide were not "caused" exclusively by socioeconomic conditions, though his not having held a full-time job for any period of time did weigh heavily on his mind. There were bigger issues at stake, namely, his realization that he was accomplishing nothing and was running out of time. In other words, he was finite and would die.

We leave lecture one, then, with the request that philosophical texts deal with life, with two suicides as exemplars of what life looks like, with the promise of pragmatism, as yet undefined, as a mediator, marrying tough-and tender-minded aspects of reality to each other. *Prag* will end with James returning to the theme of death and with his realization that it has a "tragic" dimension to it. But before we go there, let us reiterate the "manifest content" of the text, which presents pragmatism as a seemingly neutral method.

## The Middle: Pragmatism as a "Problem Solver" versus "The Will to Believe"

Pragmatism was offered by James in a manner somewhat different than it was conceived by Charles Sanders Peirce. For the latter, pragmatism was a question of determining the meaning of, say, calling a given diamond "hard" or a given knife "sharp." It would also be able to show that some issues, specifically metaphysical ones, were, in fact, meaningless. It was a matter of "dissolving" issues, so to speak.[7] For James, on the other hand, it was not a matter of showing that a given concept had no verifiable meaning but rather one of "resolving" issues, especially metaphysical ones. James says, "The pragmatic method is primarily a method of settling metaphysical disputes that otherwise might be interminable" (*Prag*, 28). Stan Thayer asks that we note the ambiguity of the term "settling" here, "which can mean *clarifying the meaning* of questions under dispute, or *resolving* the disputes by providing a satisfactory answer."[8] The new view of pragmatism offered by James focuses more on "resolution." "Meaning," that is, consistency, may be necessary, but it is not sufficient, at least not always. There is a sense of "urgency" involved that is either not found or not emphasized in Peirce. What difference does it make to me if the universe is viewed as one or as many? Is it better viewed, pragmatically speaking, as "concatenated?" What difference is there, pragmatically, between John Locke's view and George Berkeley's? None, it seems. Sometimes, as we shall see below concerning materialism versus spiritualism, the difference may seem to be more "psychological" than "logical" in nature—but James would be quick to reject this dualistic dichotomy. The history of philosophy is, after all, the clash of human temperaments. But while there is a sense of urgency here, this should not be interpreted to mean that, at some time in the future, the urgency is going to go away. In one sense, we make progress by "resolving" issues, but, in another sense, there will *always* be issues to resolve. This realization demands much of us and might even be seen as a bit pessimistic rather than naively optimistic in nature.[9]

As we have seen, James generally argues that, pragmatically speaking, an idea is true if it makes a difference, and making a difference means two things: coping with the present and preserving as much of the past as possible as one advances into the future. It is here that James gives us the metaphor of a wedding, with pragmatism as a "marrier" or minister. This is an outlook that tends to stress continuity over disruptiveness. As James says in the text, "The most violent revolutions in an individual's beliefs leave most of his old order standing. Time and space, cause and effect, nature and history, and one's own biography remain untouched" (*Prag*, 35). Such an approach is gradualist in nature and has rendered James seemingly open to criticism. As Cornel West has noted, "James's attempt to incorporate contingency and revision into a theory of truth is radical; yet in its gradualism his theory applies a Burkean notion of tradition to the production of knowledge and truth. Of course, new knowledge and truths must build on the old, but James's preoccupation with continuity minimizes disruption and precludes subversion."[10] However, while the wedding metaphor and the image of the grease spot may seem to privilege continuity over disruption, there is also evidence in the text of *Prag* that the marriage may, at least occasionally, be more disruptive than initially meets the eye. Sometimes, as the poet William Carlos Williams says:

> Divorce is
>    the sign of knowledge in our time,
>    divorce! divorce![11]

To bring this out, we turn to the issue of *pluralism,* as it appears in the text. In the fifth lecture in *Prag*, "Pragmatism and Common Sense," James argues for a topology of "regional ontologies,"[12] or multiple paradigms, with no underlying "bed of reality" to which they can be reduced. In an important passage at the end of the lecture, he says,

> There are . . . at least three well-characterized levels, stages or types of thought about the world we live in, and the notions of one stage have one kind of merit, those of another stage another kind. It is impossible, however, to say that any stage as yet in sight is absolutely more *true* than any other. Common sense is the more *consolidated* stage, because it got its innings first, and made all language into its ally. Whether it or science [the second stage] be the more *august* stage may be left to private judgment. But neither consolidation nor augustness are decisive marks of truth. . . . Vainly did scholasticism, common sense's college-trained younger sister, seek to stereotype the forms the human family had always talked with, to make them definite and fix them for eternity. . . .
>
>    There is no *ringing* conclusion possible when we compare these types of thinking, with a view to telling which is the more absolutely true. . . . Common sense is *better* for one sphere of life, science for another, philosophic criticism for a third; but whether either be *truer* absolutely, Heaven only knows. . . . Profusion, not economy, may after all be reality's key-note. (*Prag*, 92–93)

This is a pregnant paragraph. It clearly advocates both pluralism and perspectivalism as necessary accompaniments to the pragmatic method. It warns against taking common sense for granted. Contrary to common sense, it suggests that there is nothing wrong with assuming that reality may lend itself to a number of "accounts." It may be richly "profuse" rather than reducible to a final or complete picture. What, it may be asked, is the role of the philosopher, given this regional and pluralistic account? Generally, it is to articulate, preserve, and nurture the "fattest" account possible, to highlight the "thick" as opposed to the "thin" account, as James noted in lecture one, to allow each realm its due, to espouse contextualism and perspectivalism and pluralism over absolutism and certainty. One possibility might be to stress that there are "disjunctive" and "conjunctive" transitions among the domains, resulting in a more "concatenated" picture. But the phrase "levels, stages or types of thought" requires more attention. The first two suggest a rather continuous approach wherein comparison is possible. But different "types" of thinking suggest different "paradigms,"[13] if you will. Changing from one paradigm to another may be more "revolutionary" than gradualistic in nature, if common points cannot be identified. Differently stated, if there are radically different types of experience or radically different regional ontologies, then the decision as to which of them to adopt in a given situation may be disruptive or "forced." It may involve "the will to believe." For most of the time, we can adopt a gradualist approach or a concatenated one. But sometimes we are faced with experiences of different types, not reducible to one another and incompatible. This may be true on the macroscopic level of common sense versus science versus philosophy. But it may also be true on a more microscopic level of personal experiences. That is, not all experiences or situations may be of the same type, namely, solvable. Some may only be "dealt with," not solved, by exercising the will to believe. Some may be "tragic," that is, reducible neither to problems nor to will-to-believe situations.

"The will to believe" sneaks into *Prag* in the sixth lecture, "Pragmatism's Conception of Truth." There James is defending a view of truth as "agreement" but redefining agreement as other than copying. Here he tells us that we cannot "be capricious with impunity." We have to find something that will work, and that means it "must mediate between all previous truths and certain new experiences" (*Prag*, 104), keeping as much of common sense and of the past as possible. So far, all seems smooth sailing, even if the "squeeze" is a tight one. But even here, there is a rub: "Yet sometimes alternative theoretic formulas are equally compatible with all the truths we know, and then we choose between them for subjective reasons. We choose the kind of theory to which we are already partial; we follow 'elegance' or 'economy'" (ibid., 104).[14] Here, James, even though seemingly stressing the continuity model of marrying the present to the past and still allowing for the future, seems to say that there are decisions we will make where we have to color outside the lines. He seems to say that, after both sensory evidence and conceptual coherence are given their due, we will make exclusionary decisions based on "our passional nature," as he did in "the will to believe" (*WB*, 20). A pluralistic account might emphasize the fatness of the three levels, their irreducibility to an ultimate source. But a *radical* pluralism might suggest that sometimes we choose among these, running the existential risk of being wrong but, nonetheless, willing to take the chance for "personal" reasons.

A similar outcome can be seen in the issue of "materialism" versus "spiritualism" earlier in the text. James, having asked what difference it makes if one adopts one or the other, says it makes no difference concerning the past but a great deal of difference concerning the future. Spiritualism "means . . . the letting loose of hope" (*Prag*, 55). Somewhat surprisingly, the whole issue is couched in terms of "tragedy." For materialism, everything in the universe will dissolve; transient achievements will simply end, "Without an echo; without a memory; . . . This utter final wreck and tragedy is of the essence of scientific materialism as at present understood" (ibid., 54). Spiritualism, on the other hand, upholds a world "with a god in it to say the last word . . . where . . . tragedy is only provisional and partial, and shipwreck and dissolution not the absolutely final things" (ibid., 55). James here seems to say that the world of materialism does not make sense and also that tragedy can be allowed if it is only temporary. The issue is couched in terms of tragedy versus hope or partial tragedy versus complete tragedy. What does this mean? It seems to mean that, ultimately, the world has meaning, at least in the long run, that it will go on. It could be taken to mean that, ultimately, the tragic will disappear. This topic is taken up at the "end" of *Prag*.

## The End: Pragmatism and Death

Throughout the entire text of *Prag*, James has been worried that his position would be taken as a form of positivism, that is, as rejecting the claims of religion. So he returns to the issue of religion several times in the text, for example, in lectures two and three, and he devotes the entire last chapter to preserving a place for religion. He does this by offering meliorism as an alternative theory to the absolutistic or fundamentalist positions that the world is definitely damned or that it will definitely be saved: "Meliorism treats salvation as neither inevitable nor impossible. It treats it as a possibility, which becomes more and more of a probability the more numerous the actual conditions of salvation become" (*Prag*, 137). He creates the image of the world's creator, a.k.a. God, presenting an offer or challenge to all humanity, one that says that the world will be saved only on condition that each of us does his or her level best. He says that our acts are what create the world's salvation and that "Most of us . . . would . . . welcome the proposition and add our *fiat* to the *fiat* of the creator" (ibid., 140). This sort of life, for James, is a real adventure, with real danger; it is a social endeavor, of "co-operative work genuinely to be done" (ibid., 139). Here then is the challenge. And here is James perhaps exercising his own form of the will to believe—in human nature. But this optimism is tempered just a page later, in a text highlighted by Cushing Strout, who says,

> We too often forget that in his mature work, the *Pragmatism* of 1907, he [James] cried out with a tragic sense that John Dewey never had: "Is the last word sweet? Is all 'yes, yes' in the universe? Doesn't the fact of 'no' stand at the very core of life? Doesn't the very 'seriousness' that we attribute to life mean that ineluctable noes and losses form a part of it, that there are genuine sacrifices somewhere, and that something permanently drastic and bitter always remains at the bottom of its cup?"[15]

Here, at the end of *Prag,* James returns to the topic with which he began, namely, death. He admits that "in the end it is our faith and not our logic" (*Prag,* 142) that decides between affirming a dangerous and adventurous universe versus selecting absolutism. He tells the reader, "I can believe in the ideal as an ultimate, not as an origin, and as an extract, not the whole. When the cup is poured off, the dregs are left behind forever, but the possibility of what is poured off is sweet enough to accept" (ibid.). So, *Prag* begins and ends with death. James admits that our successes will be "dis-seminated and strung-along" and provides us with an image, an epigram, of one person who did *not* make it:

> A shipwrecked sailor, buried on this coast,
>    Bids you set sail.
> Full many a gallant bark, when we were lost,
>    Weathered the gale. (*Prag,* 142)

What does this mean? We have a metaphor of a dead sailor. Does the image have meaning? Can it be given meaning? Can the sailor's death be made sense of? Or is it just tragic? Theodore Roosevelt once said that "Death is always and under all circumstances a tragedy, for if it is not, then it means that life itself has become one."[16] What makes a given death tragic anyhow? The sailor's death seems to have meaning only in the sense that others "passed him by." He serves, in a Nietzschean sense, as someone whose death is a "spur" to others.[17] His death is redeemed in the successes of others, in a cooperative ongoing effort. But all this sounds more Roycian than Jamesian in character. The death of the individual sailor is meaningful, that is, makes sense "in the long run," as Peirce would say. Dewey also can be brought to bear here. In "Context and Thought," Dewey tells us that "every occurrence is a *con*currence" (*LW*, 6.9). Applied to the topic of death, my death is not my own, though it is assuredly that; it is also an event for others. As one Dewey scholar has noted, "The finality of individual death opens up the possibility, even the necessity, of participating in a shared social project which transcends individual lives—culture. Everyone dies, but culture continues."[18] Going further, in *Democracy and Education*, Dewey tells us that "Life is a self-renewing process through action upon the environment. In all the higher forms this process cannot be kept up indefinitely. After a while they succumb; they die. The creature is not equal to the task of indefinite self-renewal" (*MW*, 9.5). This quasi-Hegelian stance of not being "equal to infinity" ultimately seems to have enabled Dewey to adopt an "acceptance" model of death, that is, one that enabled him to come to terms with personal mortality by subsuming the individual self in a broader social one. Defining "life" as covering "customs, institutions, beliefs, victories and defeats, recreations and occupations," Dewey notes that "Each individual, each unit who is the carrier of the life-experience of his group, in time passes away. Yet the life of the group goes on" (ibid., 9.5).

Dewey here offers a model of individual death as "acceptable" because it is understandable "in the long run."[19] But, in James, there is much more of the personal and individual. And on a personal level, one stressing the uniqueness of the individual and the bodily, the death is perhaps more "tragic," that is, less bearable or acceptable in nature. At the very least, the "strenuous life" being offered by James as the truly pragmatic one asks a lot of us. James seems to admit as much in a response to a review of *Prag* titled "The Absolute and the Strenuous Life." He says, "The pragmatism or pluralism which I defend has to fall back on a certain ultimate hardihood, a certain willingness to live without assurances or guarantees."[20] The world of the pluralistic pragmatist "is always vulnerable, for some part may go astray; and having no 'eternal' edition of it to draw comfort from, its partisans must always feel to some degree insecure. If, as pluralists, we grant ourselves moral holidays, they can only be provisional breathing-spells, intended to refresh us for the morrow's fight. This forms one permanent inferiority of pluralism from the pragmatic point of view" (*MT*, 124). James here seems to admit that too much is being asked,[21] and that this "is bound to disappoint many sick souls whom absolutism can console" (ibid.). He seems to say that we cannot live the strenuous life all the time. Life has its "unheroic days," as Royce would say, or at least its bad moments.[22]

It may be that only some of us can live in this fashion and also that, even if we do live it, we must continually reaffirm it and that we will fail in this endeavor at least some of the time. There will be losers; in a sense, we will all lose, that is, die. Can one, in a Nietzschean sense, affirm the finitude of being human, all too human, or does this require too much? The position advanced by James in the first and last lectures on the topic of death is not one where he solves or "resolves" the issue as if it were a problem. It is, rather, a portrait or an image or an attitude that he "attests to." The intervening lectures may well concentrate on resolving issues, but the first and last lectures seem to focus on something that is not an issue or a problem, namely, individual death. Death cannot be explained by being explained away—in the long run. Or at least it is more than this. In one sense, Roosevelt is correct. Death, viewed in its immediacy, is tragic, that is, unintelligible, or is appropriated by exercising the will to believe, that is, exercising hope, unfounded hope. The question then arises of how typical is the position on the strenuous life advocated by James. Is it the rule, most of the time? Or is it the exception to the rule? Alternative paradigms might be found in Fyodor Dostoevsky's "Legend of the Grand Inquisitor" and Franz Kafka's *The Trial*, both of which seem to say that humankind cannot live without certainty or without meaning, as has been explained more fully in chapter 8. Joseph K., the antihero in *The Trial*, wants "definite acquittal" and seems unable, not just unwilling, to act without prior knowledge. As a result, he does nothing throughout the text, which consequently dissolves into a meaningless process. He dies, "like a dog," that is, on a subhuman level.[23] Dostoevsky's Grand Inquisitor confronts Christ with the accusation that most people cannot bear the freedom offered by him; they require instead "miracle, mystery, and authority."[24] Dostoevsky's "underground man" is worried that he will be "understood," perhaps even loved by Lisa. As Dostoevsky portrays him, he can preserve his freedom only by paying a terrible price—by remaining constantly "unpredictable" through spitefulness and lying.[25] In short, if James appropriates and highlights the strenuous life, Dostoevsky and Kafka remind us of how difficult it is to live it on a continual basis.[26]

## Conclusion

James "framed" the issue with which *Prag* was to deal as "the dilemma of the tough-minded vs. the tender-minded." These terms mean various things; one of them that was especially important to James was that of science versus religion. He also wanted philosophy to return to life, but life does not come in neatly disciplinary parcels. Nor does it arrive as a set of issues that can be completely solved.

Some of life's experiences are "problematic" in nature. They can be solved via the use of the pragmatic method. That method is not neutral in nature but has metaphysical presuppositions. James realizes this as he proceeds through the lectures. He also has trouble placing freedom or free will in either of the camps because freedom is more than the calculation of probabilities for him—although freedom sometimes functions in this fashion. Pragmatism as a method should be looked at within the context of the examples James brings up at the beginning and the end of the text. *Prag* begins with death, and *Prag* ends with death. Pragmatism can make some sense of death by replacing tragedy with meliorism, but there remains a sense in which death on a personal level remains inexplicable, perhaps tragic.

There are different types of experience in the universe; some of them are problematic in nature and can be "solved" via the pragmatic method. However, some of them are not problematic in nature. These include tragic situations and situations involving the will to believe. While the focus of pragmatism might seem to be on method, a method for undercutting or resolving many of the problems of traditional philosophy, we should keep in mind that not everything is a problem—or even a potential problem. This can be seen in the text itself at the beginning and at the end. Pragmatism does require pluralism and an unfinished universe. The pluralism it espouses must be one that can allow different types of experience—tragic, will-to-believe, and problematic ones. If this happens, pragmatism will never achieve the definitive triumph of a general way of thinking precisely because it will be espousing an outlook where there are only partial, that is, perspectival solutions and, sometimes, no "solutions" at all.

This realization, however, when taken with James's admission that his position would be a hard one to uphold and sustain, has resulted in that "recrudescence of absolutistic philosophies" that Dewey was so prenascent about in "The Influence of Darwin on Philosophy."[27] Pragmatism may, at first glance, have seemed to be an optimistic, progressive position, taking small steps but going forward, nonetheless. But in a sense, it has perhaps not been tried at all on a large scale. James's initial optimism about pragmatism and his efforts to show that it was not too radical but, rather, a new term for old ways of thinking were tempered as he began to realize that it seemed to demand too much of us. Specifically, it seemed to demand not only that we live with probability (uncertainty) but also with the realization and affirmation that, at least from one perspective, not everything is a problem. Specifically, neither will-to-believe-type situations nor tragic situations per se are problematic ones. In the middle of *Prag*, James comes rather close to explaining tragedy by making it temporary. But at the end of *Prag*, the shipwrecked sailor stands for not only a spur for the future but for the realization, and affirmation, that, from an individual perspective, there will also be dregs. Tragic situations cannot be solved, but they can, perhaps, be countered by offering, as an alternative, will-to-believe-type situations. Experience comes in many types; not all of them are "problematic" in nature. If the fact of "no" does "stand at the very core of life," then, on an individual personal level, we are all, in a sense, "dregs." The example or metaphor of the shipwrecked sailor, James states, requires the "acceptance of loss as unatoned for, even tho the lost element might be one's self" (*Prag,* 142). The self can be incorporated into a larger picture; consequently, death can be "accepted." But to the extent that the personal is emphasized and the uniqueness, that is, nonreplacability of the specific individual in question is stressed, to that extent, death remains inexplicable, even "tragic." Perhaps it can only be countered by constant reaffirmation through *the will to believe,* and this both unevenly and continually.

# Epilogue

Questions remain. Did James really come to realize that a complete description of reality or pure experience was not to be had?[1] That the "problem of being" could not be solved, so to speak? That one has to go on, knowing that there would be no final answer? That closure not only did not come today but indeed would never come and, hypothetically, even if it did come, we would reject it?

It would seem that pure experience cannot be defined, though it can be experienced momentarily. One must keep trying for this experience—this is what "makes a life significant," what gives life meaning. "Meaning" means "makes life worthwhile"—not just or exclusively "what makes life understandable" or "comprehensible" or "logical."

Does he realize that life cannot be described or put into words by trying to define it and failing to do so—at least not completely? Did James know, in some prenascent sense, at the very beginning, that is, around the time of "The Sentiment of Rationality," that no complete description could be attained and, if offered, would be rejected? Or did he at least hope that we would do so? "As long as one continues *talking*, intellectualism remains in undisturbed possession of the field."[2] Indeed, this is just what he did. But there is a latent and a manifest dimension to James's talk. He talks not just to describe pure experience but also to show, to disclose, indirectly, that it cannot be done. In a sense, his writings disclose two levels: first, a detailed portrayal of how things actually are and, second, a disclosure of why and how any *complete* description is both impossible and unacceptable.

Did James both yearn for and also feel repulsed by a *complete* account? A complete account would "tame" the universe. And yet no account at all would leave the universe without meaning, a "booming buzzing confusion."

James, on the face of it, seemed more worried that the universe would become too tame, too comprehensible, too domesticated. He feared that the "hawk" would turn into a "pigeon." So he worked to prevent this from occurring, stressing the unknowable, the wild, the hawk-like, etc. But he also did not want to render the universe unacceptable or unapproachable. In addition, he worried that what he was asking or proposing would require too much of us. Or at least he came to do so, shifting from describing pragmatism as merely a new word for some old ways of thinking to the realization that many people may be either unwilling or unable to reject the certainty that a more foundationalist approach offered. James remains a flawed figure—happy on the outside, afraid on the inside. He presents a manifest and a latent image to the reader. When we try to "focus" on his thought, there is a "solidity" to it, a consistent pattern describing the concrete, the contextual, the passing, the transient, etc. But there is also a latent James, one that realizes that a complete description is neither possible nor desirable—although seemingly it remains a perennial temptation.

To focus on William James, then, is a formidable task, for he discloses himself as a complicated figure. On the surface, he is the champion of heroism, the harbinger of uncertainty, of risk, of the strenuous life. But there is more to James than the espousal of the uncertain. There is also the tacit realization that certainty is, or can be, very tempting—that asking us to embrace uncertainty may indeed be asking too much from too many of us and too often over time.

Besides these two levels of James—the attack on certainty, the affirmation of risk, and, second, the temptation to accept certainty—there is, perhaps, a third level. This third level entails the realization on James's part that certainty is not coming and will not do so, ever. This is, in Paul Tillich's terms, "the courage to be."[3] It is a realization that can definitely crush the knower. "Can you live with what you know?" Progress can be made but always with the realization that there will remain more to be done—even if this realization is sometimes repressed and remains "latent."

James realized at times that "pure experience," his term for "the really real," could not be captured in concepts or language. But he did want it to be "experienced," so to speak. So he set about using language and concepts so that they had a "leading function" to perform, rather than a merely descriptive one. Concepts and words sometimes did perform a positive function, but concepts could also stifle or choke experience. Words are important—they "disclose" that part of the universe that is logical. But the universe is not all logical, and it never will be synonymous with the conceptual. The really real, whatever it is, is not only broader than the known; it is broader than the knowable, but it can be experienced at moments such as the mystical experience or the performance of the Martha Graham troupe. Realizing that the really real is broader than the knowable is difficult and demanding; it takes courage, and no one is a hero or heroine all the time.

James affirmed the self, the individual, all of his life. But that self, while heroic at times, remained a fragile one, a vulnerable self tempted by the interrelatedness of wholeness or togetherness, to try to "settle the universe's hash." James continued to make the universe meaningful by describing in great detail how people underwent their experiences in interacting with the environment, how consciousness functioned as a "stream" rather than a substance, how religious experience came via innumerable forms and so on. But the undercurrent of his thought, when focused on, discloses indirectly the harrowing and humbling fact that the universe will never be completely known. This premise is married to a second one, namely, that, even if a completely meaningful, understandable universe were offered to us, we would reject it. Is this an empirical claim or a wishful one? History is full of examples of the opposite claim, of those claiming or seeking certainty. Our century has only too many examples, old and new, of the espousal of foundationalism, absolute certainty, or unquestionable objectivity. James's claim cannot be entirely empirical—though it must have some basis in fact. But a good part of his claim is "wishful." It is, perhaps, the ultimate example of exercising "the will to believe."

James's texts are "prophetic," in the sense that Cornel West speaks of prophetic pragmatism.[4] They ask or invite us to rise to the occasion, to embrace reality "warts and all," unfinished and wild and sometimes threatening as it is. His texts, in short, ask us to act heroically, that is, to exhibit courage. Courage is usually defined as having to do with how an individual faces death. And since James constantly asks us to be courageous or heroic, we might say that James's texts are about how we deal with death.

Many texts deal with death by seeing it as part of the wider picture: "To everything there is a season." Individual death can be accepted, even embraced, if it is for the good of the group, that is, humanity at large. While this approach is understandable, it runs the danger of explaining the individual by explaining her *away*, that is, describing her in a more cosmic context. James refuses to do this.

James's texts are meant as a "spur" for us, in the same way that R. W. Emerson said that books "are for nothing but to inspire."[5] Successful texts point beyond themselves. They enable us to return to the tissue of experience. James first tried to use language in a "descriptive" fashion in *The Principles of Psychology (PP)*, *The Varieties of Religious Experience (VRE)*, and *Essays in Radical Empiricism (ERE)*. But in each case, the description turned sour and disclosed its shortcomings. James abandoned the positivism of *PP*. Psychology leaked out—into metaphysics. *VRE* offered up a sheaf of descriptive accounts of religious experience, but, ultimately, these gave way to the realization that no complete statement regarding religious experience was possible, that first-person accounts cannot be reduced to third-person statements without significant loss, that a "science of religion" is not possible. Metaphysically, the descriptive account of experience in *ERE* gives way in *A Pluralistic Universe (PU)* to the realization and affirmation that logic can only touch the surface of reality, not plumb its depths. In each case, we have a manifest account giving way to a more latent one—one stressing the role of "the will to believe."

"The will to believe" originates in James's conflict with nihilism, depression, and death, as these are found in his personal experience from 1868 to 1870 and textually written up in 1896 in the article of the same name. The will to believe is also found in one of James's last works, *PU*, published in 1909. James's philosophy is heroic and inspirational; it has to do with human mortality. It tries to affirm a universe where life "feels like a real fight," where "being" is "being heroic," at least some of the time. He tries to face death and not just accept it but rather rebel—through writing. But he realizes that death is inevitable, even if unacceptable. He tries to save himself through his texts, knowing all the time that complete closure is not possible or desirable, and embraces this, difficult as it may be to do so.

It is to be hoped that his texts will remain a "spur" for the reader, inviting her or him to return back into the concrete tissue of experience in a zestful and liberating manner.

# Notes

## 1. James's Life

1. For additional information on James's life, see the following biographies: Gay Wilson Allen, *William James* (New York: Viking Press, 1967); Daniel W. Bjork, *William James: The Center of His Vision* (New York: Columbia University Press, 1988); Linda Simon, *Genuine Reality: A Life of William James* (New York: Harcourt, Brace and Company, 1998); and Robert D. Richardson, *William James: In the Maelstrom of American Modernism* (Boston: Houghton Mifflin Company, 2006).

2. *The Letters of William James,* edited by his son, Henry James (Boston: Atlantic Monthly Press, 1920), I: 95–96.

3. Ralph Barton Perry, *The Thought and Character of William James* (Boston: Little Brown and Company, 1935), I: 322.

4. Ibid., I: 147–48. Brackets indicate that the manuscript is doubtful.

5. Bjork, *William James,* 240. In another section of the book, Bjork states, "James endured a prolonged crisis between 1898 and 1910 that distressed him as much as his time of troubles as a young man—probably more" (261).

6. Ibid., 243.

7. Charlene Haddock Seigfried, *William James's Radical Reconstruction of Philosophy* (Albany: SUNY Press, 1990).

8. William James (WJ) to Henry James (HJ), May 1865, *Correspondence* 1: 8, as quoted in Simon, *Genuine Reality,* 1998, 93.

9. WJ to HJ, May 11, 1873, as quoted in Simon, *Genuine Reality,* 135.

10. Cushing Strout, "William James and the Twice-Born Sick Soul," *Daedalus* 97, no. 3 (Summer 1968): 1069.

11. Ibid., 1073. Emphasis mine.

12. William James, "On a Certain Blindness in Human Beings," in *Talks to Teachers on Psychology and to Students on Some of Life's Ideals [TT]* (Cambridge, MA: Harvard University Press, 1983), 133.

13. Ibid., 134.

14. William James, *Essays in Philosophy [EP]* (Cambridge, MA: Harvard University Press, 1978), 4.

15. Simon, *Genuine Reality*, 296.

16. As quoted in ibid.

17. As quoted in ibid., 309.

18. As quoted in Arthur W. Frank, *The Wounded Storyteller: Body, Illness and Ethics* (Chicago: University of Chicago Press, 1995), 17.

19. Ibid., 19.

20. Ibid.

21. As quoted in Simon, *Genuine Reality*, 378.

22. Ibid., 378–79.

23. See Elisabeth Kübler-Ross, *On Death and Dying* (New York: Macmillan, 1969), passim.

24. As quoted in Simon, *Genuine Reality*, 383.

25. As quoted in ibid. See *EP*, 190.

26. *William James, A Pluralistic Universe [PU]* (Cambridge, MA: Harvard University Press, 1977), 149.

27. Quoted in Richard Rorty, *Consequences of Pragmatism* (Minneapolis: University of Minnesota Press, 1982), 174.

28. William James, *Pragmatism [Prag]* (Cambridge, MA: Harvard University Press, 1975), 142.

## 2. "The Will to Believe"

1. William James, "The Sentiment of Rationality," in *The Will to Believe and Other Essays in Popular Philosophy [WB]* (Cambridge, MA: Harvard University Press, 1979), 60. Further quotations from this work will be cited directly in the text.

2. See Thomas Kuhn, *The Structure of Scientific Revolutions* (Chicago: University of Chicago Press, 1962), 157.

3. William James, "The Will to Believe," in *WB*, 14. Further quotations from this work will be cited directly in the text.

4. Gabriel Marcel, *Being and Having: An Existentialist Diary* (New York: Harper Torch Books, Harper and Row, 1965), 96.

5. Ellen K. Suckiel, *Heaven's Champion: William James's Philosophy of Religion* (Notre Dame, IN: University of Notre Dame Press, 1996), 103.

6. Hilary Putnam, *Renewing Philosophy* (Cambridge, MA: Harvard University Press, 1992), 192.

7. Ibid.

8. Ibid.

9. See John Dewey, "The Pattern of Inquiry," in *The Writings of John Dewey*, ed. John J. McDermott (Chicago: University of Chicago Press, 1973), I: 223–39.

### 3. *The Principles of Psychology*

1. William James, *The Principles of Psychology [PP]*, (Cambridge, MA: Harvard University Press, 1981), 1: 6. All further quotations to this work will be cited in the text.

2. See ibid., 2: 962n; 1: 194n.

3. See Charlene Haddock Seigfried, *William James's Radical Reconstruction of Philosophy* (Albany: SUNY Press, 1990), ch. 7, passim.

4. Jacques Barzun, "William James and the Clue to Art," in *The Energies of Art* (New York: Vintage Press, 1962), 320. See also Jacques Barzun, *A Stroll with William James* (New York: Harper and Row, 1983), 45, 78, 101.

5. Gerald Myers, *William James: His Life and Thought* (New Haven, CT: Yale University Press, 1986), 82.

6. William James, "The Knowing of Things Together," in *Essays in Philosophy [EP]* (Cambridge, MA: Harvard University Press, 1978), 88.

### 4. *The Varieties of Religious Experience*

1. William James, *The Varieties of Religious Experience [VRE]* (Cambridge, MA: Harvard University Press, 1985), 30. All further quotations from this work will be cited in the text.

2. James, "The Will to Believe," in *The Will to Believe and Other Essays in Popular Philosophy [WB]* (Cambridge, MA: Harvard University Press, 1979), 31. One could, of course, argue that, for many people who are not religious, the universe is also a "Thou."

3. See *The Principles of Psychology [PP]* (Cambridge, MA: Harvard University Press, 1981), 1: 296: "our self feeling in this world depends entirely on what we back ourselves to be and do. It is determined by the ratio of our actualities to our supposed potentialities; a fraction of which our pretensions are the denominator and the numerator of our success: thus, Self-esteem = Success/Pretensions."

4. The reference is to Gurney's *Tertium Quid*, 1887, 99.

5. Clifford Geertz, "Deep Play: Notes on the Balinese Cockfight," in *The Interpretation of Cultures: Selected Essays*, 412–53 (New York: Basic Books, 1973), passim.

6. See Henry Samuel Levinson, *The Religious Investigations of William James* (Chapel Hill: University of North Carolina Press, 1981), 144.

7. Margaret Masterman, "The Nature of a Paradigm," in *Criticism and the Growth of Knowledge,* ed. Imre Lakatos and Alan Musgrave (Cambridge: Cambridge University Press, 1970), 79.

8. James, "A Suggestion about Mysticism," in *Essays in Philosophy [EP]* (Cambridge, MA: Harvard University Press, 1978), 165.

9. James, *A Pluralistic Universe* (Cambridge, MA: Harvard University Press, 1977), 131.

10. Ellen K. Suckiel, *Heaven's Champion: William James's Philosophy of Religion* (Notre Dame, IN: University of Notre Dame, 1996), 41.

11. Ibid., 45.

12. Ibid., 44.

### 5. Pragmatism

1. William James, *Pragmatism: A New Name for Some Old Ways of Thinking [Prag]* (Cambridge, MA: Harvard University Press, 1975), 15. All further quotations from this work will be cited in the text.

2. John E. Smith, *Purpose and Thought: The Meaning of Pragmatism* (New Haven, CT: Yale University Press, 1978), 44.

3. Alasdair MacIntyre, "Epistemological Crises, Dramatic Narrative, and the Philosophy of Science, in *Paradigms and Revolutions,* ed. Gary Gutting (Notre Dame, IN: University of Notre Dame Press, 1980), 59–60.

4. Stanley J. Scott, *Frontiers of Consciousness: Interdisciplinary Studies in American Philosophy and Poetry* (New York: Fordham University Press, 1991), 55–56.

5. Ibid., 6.

6. Charlene Haddock Seigfried, *William James's Radical Reconstruction of Philosophy* (Albany: SUNY Press, 1990), 209.

7. Ibid., 210.

### 6. Metaphysics

1. William James, *The Meaning of Truth [MT]* (Cambridge, MA: Harvard University Press, 1975), 6–7. See also William James, *Essays in Radical Empiricism [ERE]* (Cambridge, MA: Harvard University Press, 1976), 81.

2. See James, *ERE,* 29: "Whenever certain intermediaries are given, such that, as they develop toward their terminus, there is experience from point to point of one direction followed, and finally of one process fulfilled, the result is that *their starting point thereby becomes a knower and their terminus an object meant or known.*"

.

3. William James, *Pragmatism: A New Name for Some Old Ways of Thinking [Prag]* (Cambridge, MA: Harvard University Press, 1975), 107. Further quotations from this work will be cited in the text.

4. See James, *Prag,* 73ff.

5. The percept-concept distinction is particularly troublesome since James sometimes refers to reality *as* the "perceptual," even though, in other places, he says that reality includes the perceptual.

6. Paul Tillich, *Dynamics of Faith* (New York: Harper & Row, 1957), 45–46.

7. Gerald Myers, *William James: His Life and Thought* (New Haven, CT: Yale University Press, 1986), 318. It should be noted that Myers is not entirely happy with James's position here. He goes on to say, "He [James] was painting verbal pictures. . . . we should not expect more than broad brush strokes, bold analogies, suggestive metaphors, and arresting imagery. However, I do not intend to retract my . . . charge of implausibility" (ibid.).

8. See William James, *A Pluralistic Universe [PU]* (Cambridge, MA: Harvard University Press, 1977), 127. Further quotations from this work will be cited in the text.

9. Eugene Fontinell, *Self, God, and Immortality: A Jamesian Investigation* (Philadelphia: Temple University Press, 1986), 103–104. See also Fontinell's claim that "James came to realize that not everything in immediate experience was 'immediate'" (108).

10. Alfred North Whitehead, *Process and Reality* (New York: Harper Torch Books, 1929), 27ff., 44–47.

11. Gerald Myers holds that, abandoning the logic of identity over the issue of whether experiences have parts, "James moved from being a psychologist to being a philosopher, and finally to being a mystic" (*William James,* 474).

12. Sigmund Freud, *Civilization and Its Discontents,* trans. James Strachey (New York: W. W. Norton and Company, 1961), passim.

## 7. "Pure" versus "Impure" Experience

1. William James, *The Principles of Psychology [PP],* (Cambridge, MA: Harvard University Press, 1981), 1: 234. All further quotations to this work will be cited in the text.

2. Ralph Barton Perry, *The Thought and Character of William James* (Boston: Little, Brown and Co., 1935), 2: 203.

3. *The Letters of William James,* edited by his son Henry James (Boston: Atlantic Monthly Press, 1920), 1: 337–38.

4. Graham Bird, *William James* (London: Routledge & Kegan Paul, 1986), 135. See also 77.

5. See also *Prag*, 115–16: "the question 'what is *the* truth?' is no real question (being irrelative to all conditions) and the whole notion of *the* truth is an abstraction from the fact of truths in the plural, a mere useful summarizing phrase like *the* Latin Language or *the* Law." William James, *Pragmatism: A New Name for Some Old Ways of Thinking [Prag]* (Cambridge, MA: Harvard University Press, 1975). All further quotations from this work will be cited in the text.

6. Ellen K. Suckiel, *Heaven's Champion: William James's Philosophy of Religion* (Notre Dame, IN: University of Notre Dame, 1996), 43.

7. See William James, *A Pluralistic Universe [PU]* (Cambridge, MA: Harvard University Press, 1977), 60. All further quotations from this work will be cited in the text.

8. For the concept of provocation as it applies to the pragmatists, see Cornel West, *The American Evasion of Philosophy: A Genealogy of Pragmatism* (Madison: University of Wisconsin Press, 1989). See, for example, "James is the exemplary Emersonian embodiment of intellectual power, provocation, and personality" (54).

9. See William James, "The Will to Believe," in *The Will to Believe and Other Essays in Popular Philosophy [WB]* (Cambridge, MA: Harvard University Press, 1979), 6.

10. William James, *The Varieties of Religious Experience [VRE]* (Cambridge, MA: Harvard University Press, 1985), 333. All further quotations from this work will be cited in the text.

11. Suckiel, *Heaven's Champion*, 41.

12. Ibid., 44.

13. Jessica Pierce, "Unhitching the Binary via Pure Experience: A Commentary on Nishida Kitaro and William James," *The Maine Scholar* 10 (Autumn 1997): 229.

14. Ibid.

15. Nishida Kitaro, *An Inquiry Into the Good*, trans. Masao Abe and Christopher Ives (New Haven, CT: Yale University Press, 1990), 6.

16. Ibid., 10.

17. Linda Simon, *Genuine Reality: A Life of William James* (New York: Harcourt Brace, 1998), 157.

18. Ibid., 291.

## 8. Challenges to "The Will to Believe"

1. For the following, see Alfred Jules Ayer, *Language, Truth and Logic* (New York: Dover Publications, 1946), passim. Part of this present chapter was presented by the author as the Presidential Address of the William James Society in 2005 and appears in *William James Studies* 2, no. 1 (2007), as "'Problem' vs. 'Trouble': James, Kafka, Dostoevsky, and 'The Will to Believe.'"

2. A. J. Ayer, *The Origins of Pragmatism* (San Francisco: Freeman, Cooper and Company, 1968), 191. Further quotations from this work will be cited in the text.

3. See ibid., 191, 323–24.

4. See William James, *Pragmatism: A New Name for Some Old Ways of Thinking [Prag]* (Cambridge, MA: Harvard University Press, 1975), 13–26.

5. Graham Bird, *William James* (London: Routledge and Kegan Paul, 1982), 42. See also 5, 120.

6. See William James, *A Pluralistic Universe [PU]* (Cambridge, MA: Harvard University Press, 1977), 32.

7. Josiah Royce, "The Possibility of Error," in *The Philosophy of Josiah Royce,* ed. John Roth (New York: Thomas Y. Crowell Company, 1971), 44.

8. Josiah Royce, "Loyalty and Religion," in *The Philosophy of Josiah Royce,* 329. Further quotations from this work will be cited in the text.

9. Franz Kafka, *The Trial* (New York: Schocken Books, 1968), 229.

10. Hilary Putnam, *Renewing Philosophy* (Cambridge, MA: Harvard University Press, 1992), 191.

11. See Robert B. Talisse and D. Micah Hester, *On James* (Belmont, CA: Wodsworth-Thompson Learning, 2004), 90.

12. Fyodor Dostoevsky, *Notes from the Underground and the Grand Inquisitor,* selection, translation, and introduction by Ralph Matlaw (New York: E. P. Dutton, 1960), 115.

13. William James, "The Will to Believe," in *The Will to Believe and Other Essays in Popular Philosophy [WB]* (Cambridge, MA: Harvard University Press, 1979), 33.

14. Robert Lord, "Descent from Reality," in *Dostoevsky: Essays and Perspectives* (Berkeley: University of California Press, 1970), 35.

15. See William James, *The Varieties of Religious Experience* (Cambridge, MA: Harvard University Press, 1985), 134.

16. *The Writings of William James,* ed. John J. McDermott (New York: Modern Library, Random House, 1967), xxi.

17. See Phil Oliver, *William James's "Springs of Delight": The Return of Life* (Nashville, TN: Vanderbilt University Press, 2001), 15, 46–49.

18. See *Prag,* 35.

19. John McDermott, "Why Bother? Is Life Worth Living?" *Journal of Philosophy* 88, no. 11 (1991): 683.

## Conclusion

1. William James, *Pragmatism: A New Name for Some Old Ways of Thinking [Prag]* (Cambridge, MA: Harvard University Press, 1975), 21. All further quotations from this work will be cited in the text. Most of this chapter originally ap-

peared as *"Pragmatism* and Death: Method vs. Metaphor, Tragedy vs. the Will to Believe," in *100 Years of Pragmatism: William James's Revolutionary Philosophy,* ed. John J. Stuhr, 81–95 (Bloomington: Indiana University Press, 2010).

2. See *James, Prag,* 22.

3. See John Dewey, "The Pattern of Inquiry" [Late Works], 12.105ff. All references to Dewey's work are to *The Collected Works of John Dewey,* ed. Jo Ann Boydston (Carbondale and Edwardsville: Southern Illinois Press, 1969–91), and published as *Early Works, Middle Works, and Late Works.* Hereafter referred to as *EW, MW,* and *LW.*

4. On this topic, see John Stuhr, "Persons, Pluralism, and Death: Towards a Disillusioned Pragmatism," in *Genealogical Pragmatism: Philosophy, Experience, and Community* (Albany: SUNY Press, 1997), 277–95.

5. Kathleen Higgins, *Nietzsche's Zarathustra* (Philadelphia: Temple University Press, 1987), 19.

6. For the notion of "exemplar," see Thomas Kuhn, *The Structure of Scientific Revolutions,* 2nd ed. (Chicago: University of Chicago Press, 1970), 187–91.

7. See Robert Talisse and D. Micah Hester, *On James* (Belmont, CA: Wadsworth, 2004), 44.

8. H. S. Thayer, *Meaning and Action: A Study of American Pragmatism* (Indianapolis: Bobbs-Merrill, 1973), 77, footnote.

9. Talisse and Hester catch this point well in their book *On James:* "While not strictly pessimistic, it may seem that James has painted a thoroughly bleak picture of human life: We are caught in a fight that we cannot win; we must participate in an ongoing struggle between good and evil, but we have not the resources to secure a decisive victory; we are called to commit to the meliorist project of improving the world, but we have no guarantee that even our very best efforts can succeed. What kind of life is this?" (71).

10. Cornel West, *The American Evasion of Philosophy: A Genealogy of Pragmatism* (Madison: University of Wisconsin Press, 1989), 65.

11. William Carlos Williams, *Paterson* (New York: New Directions, 1946–58), 18.

12. For the notion of "regional ontology," see Edmund Husserl, *Ideas,* trans. W. R. Boyce Gibson (New York: Collier Books, Macmillan, 1962), 57ff.

13. For the notion of paradigm, see Thomas Kuhn, *The Structure of Scientific Revolutions,* passim.

14. See also William James, "The Will to Believe," in *The Will to Believe and Other Essays in Popular Philosophy [WB]* (Cambridge, MA: Harvard University Press, 1979), 13–33. Further quotations from this work will be cited in the text.

15. Cushing Strout, "William James and the Twice-Born Sick Soul," *Daedalus* 97, no. 3 (Summer 1968): 1079. Original reference is to *Prag,* 141.

16. Theodore Roosevelt, "Letter to Cecil Spring-Rice," March 12, 1900, in *The Works of Theodore Roosevelt,* ed. H. Hagedorm (New York: Charles Scribner's Sons, 1926), 2: 102; as quoted in Stuhr, "Persons, Pluralism and Death," 278.

17. For the notions of "dying at the right time" and death as a "spur," see Friedrich Nietzsche, *Thus Spoke Zarathustra,* trans. R. J. Hollingdale (New York: Penguin Books, 1961), 97–99.

18. Thomas Alexander, *John Dewey's Theory of Art, Experience and Nature: The Horizons of Feeling* (Albany: SUNY Press, 1987), 159.

19. For a very different view of Dewey, one emphasizing that "self-realization is self-depletion," see Stuhr, "Persons, Pluralism, and Death," 277–95.

20. William James, *The Meaning of Truth [MT]* (Cambridge, MA: Harvard University Press, 1975), 124. Further quotations from this work will be cited in the text.

21. As John Stuhr has noted, in the years following the publication of *Prag,* "James increasingly and insightfully recognized that pragmatism, immensely right in theory, was unlikely to be a 'definitive triumph' in life because it constituted in practice a philosophy that is insufficiently a live option or is a far too demanding and strenuous an option for many persons." "Pragmatism, Pluralism, and the Future of Philosophy: Farewell to an Idea," in John Stuhr, *Pragmatism, Postmodernism, and the Future of Philosophy* (New York and London: Routledge, 2003), 172.

22. See Josiah Royce, *The Religious Aspect of Philosophy* (Boston: Houghton Mifflin Company, 1885), 385.

23. See Franz Kafka, *The Trial* (New York: Schocken Books, 1968).

24. See this episode in Fyodor Dostoevsky, *Notes from the Underground and the Grand Inquisitor,* selection, translation and introduction by Ralph Matlaw (New York: E. P. Dutton, 1960), 117–41.

25. See ibid., 3–115.

26. See William J. Gavin, "'Problem' vs. 'Trouble': James, Kafka, Dostoevsky and 'The Will to Believe,'" *William James Studies* 2, no. 1 (October 2007): http:// williamjamesstudies.org/2.1/gavin.html.

27. See Dewey, *MW,* 4.13.

## Epilogue

1. Phil Oliver has astutely noted that "James . . . would have done us all a service if he had spoken not of pure experience but rather of pure experiences." Phil Oliver, *William James's "Springs of Delight": The Return to Life* (Nashville, TN: Vanderbilt University Press, 2001), 91.

2. *William James, A Pluralistic Universe* (Cambridge, MA: Harvard University Press, 1977), 131.

3. See Paul Tillich, *The Courage to Be* (New Haven, CT: Yale University Press, 1952), passim. See also Robert J. O'Connell, *William James on the Courage to Believe* (New York: Fordham University Press, 1984), passim.

4. See Cornel West, "Prophetic Pragmatism: Cultural Criticism and Political Engagement," in *The American Evasion of Philosophy* (Madison: University of Wisconsin Press, 1989), 211–39.

5. Ralph Waldo Emerson, "The American Scholar," in *Selected Writings of Ralph Waldo Emerson*, edited with a foreword by William H. Gilman (New York: New American Library, 1965), 228.

# Bibliography

Alexander, Thomas. *John Dewey's Theory of Art, Experience and Nature: The Horizons of Feeling*. Albany: SUNY Press, 1987.

Allen, Gay Wilson. *William James*. New York: Viking, 1967.

Ayer, A. J. *Language, Truth and Logic*. New York: Dover Publications Inc., 1946.

———. *The Origins of Pragmatism*. San Francisco: Freeman, Cooper & Company, 1968.

Barzun, Jacques. *A Stroll with William James*. New York: Harper and Row, 1983.

———. "William James and the Clue to Art." In *The Energies of Art*, 320–50. New York: Vintage Books, 1962.

Bird, Graham. *William James*. London: Routledge & Kegan Paul, 1986.

Bjork, Daniel. *William James: The Center of His Vision*. New York: Columbia University Press, 1988.

Bordogna, Francesca. *William James at the Boundaries: Philosophy, Science, and the Geography of Knowledge*. Chicago: University of Chicago Press, 2008.

Coktin, George. *William James, Public Philosopher*. Baltimore, MD: Johns Hopkins University Press, 1990.

Cooper, Wesley. *The Unity of William James's Thought*. Nashville, TN: Vanderbilt University Press, 2002.

Cormier, Harvey. *The Truth Is What Works: William James, Pragmatism, and the Seed of Death*. Lanham, MD: Rowman & Littlefield, 2000.

Dewey, John. *The Collected Works of John Dewey, 1882–1953*. Edited by Jo Ann Boydston. 37 vols. Carbondale and Edwardsville: Southern Illinois Press, 1969–91. Published as *The Early Works: 1882–1898 (EW)*, *The Middle Works: 1899–1924 (MW)*, and *The Later Works: 1925–1953 (LW)*.

———. "The Pattern of Inquiry." In *The Writings of John Dewey,* ed. John J. McDermott, 223–39. Chicago: University of Chicago Press, 1973.

Dostoevsky, Fyodor. *Notes from the Underground and the Grand Inquisitor.* Selection, translation, and introduction by Ralph Matlaw. New York: E. P. Dutton, 1960.

Emerson, Ralph Waldo. "The American Scholar." In *Selected Writings of Ralph Waldo Emerson,* edited and with a foreword by William H. Gilman, 223–40. New York: New American Library, 1965.

Feinstein, Howard. *Becoming William James.* Ithaca, NY: Cornell University Press, 1984.

Fontinell, Eugene. *Self, God, and Immortality: A Jamesian Investigation.* Philadelphia: Temple University Press, 1986.

Frank, Arthur W. *The Wounded Storyteller: Body, Illness and Ethics.* Chicago: University of Chicago Press, 1995.

Freud, Sigmund. *Civilization and Its Discontents.* Translated by James Strachey. New York: W. W. Norton, 1961.

Gale, Richard. *The Divided Self of William James.* Cambridge: Cambridge University Press, 1999.

Gavin, William. "'Problem' vs. 'Trouble': James, Kafka, Dostoevsky and 'The Will to Believe.'" *William James Studies* 2, no. 1 (2007): http://williamjamesstudies.org/2.1/gavin.html.

———. *William James and the Reinstatement of the Vague.* Philadelphia: Temple University Press, 1992.

Geertz, Clifford. "Deep Play: Notes on the Balinese Cockfight." In *The Interpretation of Cultures: Selected Essays,* 412–53. New York: Basic Books, 1973.

Goodman, Russell. *Wittgenstein and William James.* Cambridge: Cambridge University Press, 2002.

Higgins, Kathleen. *Nietzsche's Zarathustra.* Philadelphia: Temple University Press, 1987.

Husserl, Edmund. *Ideas.* Translated by W. R. Boyce Gibson. New York: Collier Books, Macmillan Publishing, 1962.

James, William. *The Letters of William James, edited by his son Henry James.* Boston: Atlantic Monthly Press, 1920.

Kafka, Franz. *The Trial.* New York: Schocken Books, 1968.

Kübler-Ross, Elisabeth. *On Death and Dying.* New York: Macmillan, 1969.

Kuhn, Thomas. *The Structure of Scientific Revolutions.* Chicago: University of Chicago Press, 1962; 2nd. ed., 1970.

Levinson, Henry Samuel. *The Religious Investigations of William James.* Chapel Hill: University of North Carolina Press, 1981.

Lord, Robert. "Descent from Reality." In *Dostoevsky: Essays and Perspectives,* 35–47. Berkeley: University of California Press, 1970.

MacIntyre, Alasdair. "Epistemological Crises, Dramatic Narrative, and the Philosophy of Science." In *Paradigms and Revolutions,* edited by Gary Gutting, 54–74. Notre Dame, IN: University of Notre Dame Press, 1980.

Marcel, Gabriel. *Being and Having: An Existentialist Diary.* New York: Harper Torch Books, Harper and Row, 1965.

Masterman, Margaret. "The Nature of a Paradigm." In *Criticism and the Growth of Knowledge,* ed. Imre Lakatos and Alan Musgrave, 59–89. Cambridge: Cambridge University Press, 1970.

McDermott, John J. "Why Bother? Is Life Worth Living?" *Journal of Philosophy* 88, no. 11 (1991): 667–83.

———, ed. *The Writings of William James.* New York: Modern Library Random House, 1967.

Myers, Gerald. *William James: His Life and Thought.* New Haven, CT: Yale University Press, 1986.

Nietzsche, Friedrich. *Thus Spoke Zarathustra. Translated and with an introduction by R. J. Hollingdale.* New York: Penguin Books, 1961.

Nishida, Kitaro. *An Inquiry Into the Good.* Translated by Masao Abe and Christopher Ives. New Haven, CT: Yale University Press, 1990.

O'Connell, Robert J., S.J. *William James on the Courage to Believe.* New York: Fordham University Press, 1984.

Oliver, Phil. *William James's "Springs of Delight": The Return to Life.* Nashville, TN: Vanderbilt University Press, 2001.

Perry, Ralph Barton. *The Thought and Character of William James.* 2 vols. Boston: Little Brown, 1935.

Pierce, Jessica. "Unhitching the Binary via Pure Experience: A Commentary on Nishida Kitaro and William James." *The Maine Scholar* 10 (Autumn 1997): 229–35.

Putnam, Hilary. *Renewing Philosophy.* Cambridge, MA: Harvard University Press, 1992.

Putnam, Ruth Anna, ed. *The Cambridge Companion to William James.* Cambridge: Cambridge University Press, 1997.

Richardson, Robert D. *William James: In the Maelstrom of American Modernism.* Boston: Houghton Mifflin, 2006.

Rorty, Richard. *Consequences of Pragmatism.* Minneapolis: University of Minnesota Press, 1982.

Roth, John, ed. *The Philosophy of Josiah Royce.* New York: Thomas Y. Crowell Company, 1971.

Royce, Josiah. *The Religious Aspect of Philosophy.* Boston: Houghton Mifflin Company, 1885.

Scott, Stanley J. *Frontiers of Consciousness: Interdisciplinary Studies in American Philosophy and Poetry.* New York: Fordham University Press, 1991.

Seigfried, Charlene Haddock. *William James's Radical Reconstruction of Philosophy.* Albany: SUNY Press, 1990.

Simon, Linda. *Genuine Reality: A Life of William James.* New York: Harcourt Brace, 1998.

Smith, John E. *Purpose and Thought: The Meaning of Pragmatism.* New Haven, CT: Yale University Press, 1978.

Strout, Cushing. "William James and the Twice-Born Sick Soul." *Daedalus* 97, no. 3 (Summer 1968): 1062–82.

Stuhr, John J. *Genealogical Pragmatism: Philosophy, Experience, and Community.* Albany: SUNY Press, 1997.

———. *Pragmatism, Postmodernism, and the Future of Philosophy.* New York and London: Routledge, 2003.

———, ed. *100 Years of Pragmatism: William James's Revolutionary Philosophy.* Bloomington: Indiana University Press, 2010.

Suckiel, Ellen K. *Heaven's Champion: William James's Philosophy of Religion.* Notre Dame, IN: University of Notre Dame Press, 1996.

———. *The Pragmatic Philosophy of William James.* Notre Dame, IN: University of Notre Dame Press, 1984.

Talisse, Robert B., and D. Micah Hester. *On James.* Belmont, CA: Wadsworth, 2004.

Thayer, H. S. *Meaning and Action: A Study of American Pragmatism.* Indianapolis: Bobbs-Merrill, 1973.

Tillich, Paul. *The Courage to Be.* New Haven, CT: Yale University Press, 1952.

———. *Dynamics of Faith.* New York: Harper & Row, 1957.

West, Cornel. *The American Evasion of Philosophy: A Genealogy of Pragmatism.* Madison: University of Wisconsin Press, 1989.

Whitehead, Alfred North. *Process and Reality.* New York: Harper Torch Books, 1929.

Wild, John. *The Radical Empiricism of William James.* Garden City, NJ: Doubleday, 1969.

Williams, William Carlos. *Paterson.* New York: New Directions, 1946–58.

# Index

WILLIAM J. GAVIN is Professor of Philosophy at the University of Southern Maine where he has taught for over forty years. He is the author of more than one hundred articles and reviews, many of them dealing with the work of William James and American philosophy in general. Among his books are *William James and the Reinstatement of the Vague* and *Cuttin' the Body Loose: Historical, Biological, and Personal Approaches in Death and Dying.* He is former president of the William James Society.